RAND NATIONAL SECURITY RESEARCH DIVISION

Markets for Cybercrime Tools and Stolen Data

Hackers' Bazaar

Lillian Ablon, Martin C. Libicki, Andrea A. Golay

Sponsored by Juniper Networks

The research described in this report was sponsored by Juniper Networks and conducted within the Acquisition and Technology Policy Center of the RAND National Security Research Division.

The RAND Corporation is a nonprofit institution that helps improve policy and decisionmaking through research and analysis. RAND's publications do not necessarily reflect the opinions of its research clients and sponsors.

Support RAND—make a tax-deductible charitable contribution at www.rand.org/giving/contribute.html

RAND® is a registered trademark.

RAND OFFICES
SANTA MONICA, CA • WASHINGTON, DC
PITTSBURGH, PA • NEW ORLEANS, LA • JACKSON, MS • BOSTON, MA
CAMBRIDGE, UK • BRUSSELS, BE
www.rand.org

Preface

Markets are good because they facilitate economic efficiency, but when that efficiency facilitates criminal activity, such "black markets" can be deemed harmful. Criminal activities in cyberspace are increasingly facilitated by burgeoning black markets in both the tools (e.g., exploit kits) and the take (e.g., credit card information). As with most things, intent is what can make something criminal or legitimate, and there are cases where goods or services can be used for altruistic or malicious purposes (e.g., bulletproof hosting and zero-day vulnerabilities).

This report describes the fundamental characteristics of these markets and how they have grown into their current state in order to give insight into how their existence can harm the information security environment. Understanding the current and predicted landscape for these markets lays the groundwork for follow-on exploration of options that could minimize the potentially harmful influence these markets impart. This report assumes the reader has a basic understanding of the cyber, criminal, and economic domains, but includes a glossary to supplement any gaps.

This report should be of interest to cybersecurity, information security, and law enforcement communities. It was sponsored by Juniper Networks as part of a multiphase study on the future security environment.

This research was conducted within the Acquisition and Technology Policy (ATP) Center of the RAND National Security Research Division (NSRD). NSRD conducts research and analysis on defense and national security topics for the U.S. and allied defense, foreign policy, homeland security, and intelligence communities and foundations and other nongovernmental organizations that support defense and national security analysis.

For more information on the ATP Center, see http://www.rand.org/nsrd/ndri/centers/atp.html or contact the director (contact information is provided on the web page).

Comments or questions on this report should be addressed to the lead author, Lillian Ablon, at Lily_Ablon@rand.org, or the project leader, Martin Libicki, at Martin_Libicki@rand.org.

Contents

Figures and Tables

Figures

Tables

Summary

Black and gray markets for hacking tools, hacking services, and the fruits of hacking are gaining widespread attention as more attacks and attack mechanisms are linked in one way or another to such markets. In the December 2013 breach of the retail giant Target, where data from as many as 40 million credit cards and 70 million user accounts were hijacked, such data appeared within days on black-market sites. Other examples of attacks and their links to underground markets include

- recent increases in the use of watering-hole attacks (where users visit popular, legitimate, but compromised websites) based on well-known exploit kits available for sale on the black market (see, e.g., Malwageddon, 2013)
- the growing prevalence of malware inserted into online advertisements that, when clicked, infect a victim's computer, and call back to an exploit kit to launch additional malware; data is then stolen and sold on black markets (e.g., Joostbijl, 2014)
- websites throttled by Distributed Denial of Service (DDoS) attacks implemented by rented botnets available on the black market (e.g., Schwartz, 2010).

These black markets are growing in size and complexity. The hacker market—once a varied landscape of discrete, ad hoc networks of individuals initially motivated by little more than ego and notoriety—has emerged as a playground of financially driven, highly organized, and sophisticated groups. In certain respects, the black market can be more profitable than the illegal drug trade; the links to end-users are more direct, and because worldwide distribution is accomplished electronically, the requirements are negligible.

Understanding this market in its entirety is complicated by the fact that it is geographically spread out, diverse, segmented, and usually hidden under the cloak of darknets (e.g., Tor), anonymization, and cryptographic features. What can be surmised from interviews with expert observers is that the hacker market poses a formidable challenge and an increasing threat to businesses, governments, and individuals operating in the digital world.

Increasing sophistication and specialization characterizes both how the market operates and the types of goods and services being sold. As with any other market, products and vendors tend to be reliable; but the unwary can be scammed or sold products with unwanted features. Methods for communication have gotten more innovative and secure: there is greater use of encryption and privacy mechanisms, such as off-the-record messaging and digital and cryptocurrencies. Organization of groups and forums are highly structured, and specialization of roles and responsibilities is common. Vendors often guarantee their products' lifespan or value, and some track what a customer does with their product—a hacker's version of "digital rights management."

There has been a steady increase in the availability of goods and services offered, from stolen records and exploit kits to "stolen-to-order" goods, such as intellectual property and zero-day (more commonly, half-day) vulnerabilities. Greater availability of as-a-service models, point-and-click tools, and easy-to-find online tutorials makes it easier for technical novices to use what these markets have to offer. Despite these markets being generally illicit, they follow the same economic laws and practices as other markets: Participants communicate through various channels, place their orders, and get products. Black-market evolution mirrors the normal evolution of a free market, with both innovation and growth. Prices for credit cards, for example, are falling because the market is flooded with records, and botnets and DDoS capabilities are cheaper because so many more options are available.

Access to such markets, conversely, is getting tighter. Motivated, in part, by recent black market takedowns, more sophisticated markets are undertaking more rigorous and aggressive vetting of individuals. More transactions are taking place on virtual private networks and darknets, with anonymization and encryption capabilities enabled.

Despite increased efforts by law enforcement to disrupt and shut down various parts of the market—from its financing to popular marketplaces—the hacker economy has proved to be quite resilient. The market bounces back after a takedown or arrest. Finding comparable replacements for market leaders like the Blackhole Exploit Kit or the Silk Road may take a few iterations, but substitutes appear almost immediately as competing forums constantly vie for market share. That said, law enforcement is getting better for a number of reasons: More individuals are technologically savvy; suspects are going after bigger targets, and thus are attracting more attention; and more crimes involve a digital component, giving law enforcement more opportunities to encounter crime in cyberspace.

Adding to the complexity for defenders are the rapidly emerging and highly secretive markets for zero-day vulnerabilities, which occur in both gray (licit) and black (illicit) markets. Discussions surrounding zero-days have risen in prominence because of increased media attention and recent decisions by many software makers to pay for discoveries of such vulnerabilities. Ironically, sources of information that were once forthcoming have gone silent of late.

Noteworthy Projections and Predictions

Since the mid-2000s, the hacking community has been steadily growing and maturing, as has its market. It took more than a decade of continuous development and innovation, the introduction of new generations of digitally savvy participants, and significant trial and error to achieve today's landscape, in which experts agree on the following projections and predictions:

- There will be more activity in darknets, more checking and vetting of participants, more use of cryptocurrencies, greater anonymity capabilities in malware, and more attention to encrypting and protecting communications and transactions.
- Helped by such markets, the ability to attack will likely outpace the ability to defend.
- Hyperconnectivity will create more points of presence for attack and exploitation, so that crime will increasingly have a networked or cyber component, creating a wider range of opportunities for black markets.

- Exploitation of social networks and mobile devices will continue to grow.
- There will be more hacking for hire, as-a-service offerings, and brokers.

Experts disagree, however, on who will be most affected by the growth of the black market (e.g., small or large businesses, individuals), what products will be on the rise (e.g., fungible goods, such as data records and credit card information; nonfungible goods, such as intellectual property), or which types of attacks will be most prevalent (e.g., persistent, targeted attacks; opportunistic, mass "smash-and-grab" attacks).

For Further Research

The harmful effects of black markets on cybersecurity suggest the need for options to suppress such market activity—without which, very little is likely to change. The search for such options raises several questions. How should security technologies and law enforcement shift their approaches to thwart the rise of the markets? How might bug bounty programs or better pay and incentives from legitimate companies shift transactions and talent off the illicit markets into legitimate business operations? Would it be worthwhile to establish fake credit card shops, fake forums, and sites for counterfeit goods that would flood the market with fake items? Would more vigorous law enforcement help? Would international cooperation be required to put muscle behind today's law enforcement? Should there be mandates for encryption on point-of-sale terminals, safer and stronger storage of passwords and user credentials, implementation of "chip and PIN" (personal identification number) in the United States? If companies do not comply, would making them liable for data breaches decrease activity on the markets?

Such questions are candidates for further research.

Acknowledgments

RAND reports typically draw on a wide collection of supporters, collaborators, and helpers in their creation. We would first like to mention the invaluable insights provided by the numerous security experts at Juniper Networks. Within RAND, Cynthia Cook and Henry Willis have been wise and patient in their assistance and insight to this project. Our reviewers, Ed Balkovich and Igor Mikolic-Torreira, offered sage advice that improved the report. Jerry Sollinger gave generously of his time to help format and edit multiple drafts.

Finally, we are exceptionally grateful to all those who took the time to share their knowledge of black and gray markets, including those who offered their wisdom anonymously and those mentioned in the bibliography.

Abbreviations

DDoS	Distributed Denial of Service
GPG	GNU Privacy Guard
I2P	Invisible Internet Project
IP	intellectual property
IRC	Internet Relay Chat
P2P	peer-to-peer
PHI	protected health information
PII	personally identifiable information
PIN	personal identification number
R&D	research and development
SMS	Short Message Service
VPN	virtual private network

CHAPTER ONE

Introduction and Research Methodology

Markets tend to make activities more efficient, whether such activities are laudable or criminal (or, at least, subterranean). The world of hacking can be seen as a market: Buyers seek the best price; sellers ply their wares or skills to make the most profit. This scenario is subject to typical market forces, with prices rising when demand is high and falling when it is low. Over time, good products squeeze out bad ones, and high-quality brands can command premium prices. Mergers and acquisitions occur, and deals get made between market participants who know and trust each other. Innovation is constant, and new products thrive or wither depending on the judgment of the market.

Over the last ten to 15 years, an activity that had typically been carried out by individuals working alone has evolved to one done by organizations and aided by the exchange of goods and services among organizations and individuals. To the extent that such exchanges increase the efficiency of computer network attack and exploitation, they multiply the challenges faced by companies, governments, and others with information to steal.

During the busy 2013 holiday shopping season, point-of-sale terminals at retail giant Target were infected by malicious hackers, resulting in the compromise of at least 70 million customer records, including customer names, debit and credit card numbers, expiration dates, and security codes. Within days, these customer records started to appear on underground forums—or hacker black markets. This is just one of many data breaches with the intent to sell the spoils on the black market, and is a timely reminder that the market for stolen information is very much alive and thriving, as is the market for the services used to obtain that information.

Our goal in investigating such markets was to understand their character and the trends in their development. In doing so, we separate what we call black markets from gray ones, although such markets may overlap. Black markets are organized and run for the purpose of cybercrime;[1] they deal in exploit kits, botnets, Distributed Denial of Service (DDoS), attack services, and the fruits of crime (e.g., stolen credit card numbers, compromised hosts). Gray markets, by our definition, are limited to the exchange of vulnerabilities and exploits, the discovery and development of which are not illegal per se (legitimate companies, for instance, often pay for information about vulnerabilities in their own products), but can nevertheless be

---

[1] One way to subdivide cybercriminals with varying intent is as follows:
- individuals or small groups: intent is for financial gain
- organized criminals: intent is for financial gain
- nation-states: intent is to monitor, exploit, or attack threats
- cyberterrorists: intent is to degrade, destroy, disrupt, deny, or deceive
- hactivists: intent is for notoriety or visibility.

troubling because they also complicate the life of system defenders. As more news and reports cover this topic, gray markets and transactions have become more acceptable, although controversy remains (e.g., Egelman, 2013).

We conducted this research primarily through more than two dozen interviews with subject-matter experts, carried out between October and December 2013. These experts included academics, security researchers, reporters, security vendors, and law enforcement, each bringing a unique perspective. We identified these experts through a variety of methods: Some had written reports, papers, or articles, given talks or presentations on the topic; others were individuals with whom we had a personal connection and who had experience in this realm; some were contacts provided by our sponsor. Additionally, some interviewees referred us to other experts. In all, we received approximately a 35-percent response rate.

Although we sought details, we could not avoid generalities. Many experts did not want to give details lest they interfere with ongoing investigations, alert criminals to what the security industry knows, compromise current clients of security vendors, or provide a "how-to handbook" for getting involved in the black market. Almost a quarter of the experts spoke on condition of anonymity. Where appropriate, we distinguish which views are held by multiple experts or just one.

Secondarily, we reviewed literature related to this topic, including news articles, conference talks, books, and reports. The bibliography provides a full listing.

The results are suggestive, but the nature of the market means they are not definitive. Criminals try to hide what they do; their markets are clandestine by nature, and statistics on them are imprecise. Experts can disagree even on very basic points.

With such caveats in mind, we start with black markets. We review their primary characteristics: their structure, operating conduits, participants, products, and pricing. We also discuss the role that reliability and integrity play, and the markets' sensitivity to external events and resilience. We then touch on two special areas of interest: botnets and zero-day vulnerabilities. The former is one of the largest enablers of cybercrime, while the latter has a place in both black and gray markets, and has gotten increased attention lately. We then focus on indicators of the maturity of the black market, and what are seen as the most likely and noteworthy projections and predictions. We end with our conclusions, and include an appendix showing a timeline of relevant events leading to the current market, as well as a glossary of terms to supplement the reader's understanding of the cyber, criminal, and economic domains.

CHAPTER TWO

Characteristics of the Black Market

Black markets emerged as it became increasingly obvious that a lot of money could be made for relatively low investment. The growth of the Internet allowed like-minded individuals to find each other and connect more easily, providing easier access to tools and weapons, as well as to more targets. Barriers to entry were low for those with appropriate access and vetting. The risk was also low (compared with other criminal markets), at least initially, because law enforcement was ill equipped to track it (although they are increasingly getting more effective). The slow adaptation of law to the demands of cyberspace has made for a difficult (and often slow) fight for law enforcement.[1]

The black market is not so much a market as it is a collection of activities that range from simple to extremely sophisticated and operate all over the world, from New Jersey to Nigeria to China and Southeast Asia. Goods and services tend to be reliable (though not always), and implementation and transactions are quick and efficient. These markets are compared by some to underground markets for other illicit goods, such as drugs, with the difference that digital goods carry less risk and can offer greater profit.

When we say *market(s)*, we mean the collection of (skilled and unskilled) suppliers, vendors, potential buyers, and intermediaries for goods or services surrounding digitally based crimes.[2] A *marketplace* is the location in which a market operates—in our case, it is typically virtual or digital.

It is challenging to describe what the entire market looks like. It is too vast, has too many players, is too disjointed, is constantly changing, and, because it is a criminal market, pains are taken to prevent law enforcement from understanding it. People often only have a good handle on their own niche, geography, or product. The remainder of this section delves into the various components of the black market (structure, participants, operating conduits, products, pricing) and provides some commentary on the market's reliability and integrity, sensitivity to external events, and resilience to takedowns. We will paint as encompassing a picture as possible, given the scarcity of available details.

---

[1] Take, for example, the case of sentencing a high-ranking member of CarderPlanet—almost a decade after his arrest (Farivar, 2013).

[2] A few of these crimes include financial (e.g., account compromise, account credentials, credit card data), nonfinancial (e.g., credentials for eCommerce, social media, gaming), intellectual property (IP) theft, counterfeit goods, defamation, or takedown of sites.

Structure

Hacker markets have evolved over time and now come in many forms. In the early to mid-2000s, they focused on goods and services surrounding credit card data. Then, they expanded to broker credentials for eCommerce accounts, social media, and beyond. These days, some are still dedicated to one product or a specialized service, while others offer a range of goods and services for a full lifecycle of an attack; some are "storefronts" that offer many products but not complete one-stop shopping. Some vendors advertise on multiple marketplaces; others stick to just a few online forums. Even within single forums or stores, there are different tiers of access for various products. Some underground organizations can reportedly reach 70,000–80,000 people, with a global footprint that brings in hundreds of millions of dollars (e.g., carder.su, a now-defunct forum that was dedicated to all aspects of credit card fraud). These market-places—particularly the harder-to-access tiers where participants are highly vetted—are often well structured and policed, with their own constitution-like rules and guidelines to follow. That said, plenty of the market does not have rules and regulations—one reason experts say the black market can outpace the legitimate world.

Criminals of multiple skill levels can participate in the black market because targets vary in their hardness (as far as stealing data is concerned, some say individuals tend to be softer or easier targets than organizations). Most players go after any exploitable device, employing "smash-and-grab" techniques, using goods acquired in the more easily accessible channels. Fewer players are good enough to target specific systems, companies, or victims.[3] These more sophisticated, more focused attackers require access to higher tiers or to in-house research and development (R&D) for the most advanced tools and expertise. Those who would carry out targeted attacks may explore peer-to-peer solicitations rather than the more open public forums or chat channels to acquire their desired goods and services. But players of various skill levels often support one another. For example, highly skilled players, through a breach, may capture IP along with data or account credentials. They may then sell the IP to those who deal in corporate espionage, and the data and credentials to other, potentially less-skilled individuals for further exploitation and sale.

But almost any computer-literate person can enter the market. With the increase of as-a-service models and do-it-yourself kits (with easy-to-use administration panels), anyone can create and use variants of similar malware. One can buy credentials, credit cards, and personally identifiable information (PII) without needing to be highly technical. This is increasingly true for those involved in identity theft.

One expert estimates that in the mid-2000s, approximately 80 percent of black-market participants were freelance (the rest being part of criminal organizations or groups), but has declined and is closer to 20 percent today.[4] These freelancers span markets and tiers of varying access. But while an individual is good at one thing, organizations (or well-coordinated

---

[3]   One expert suggested that true targeted attacks are about 5 percent of the market, and the remaining 95 percent are consumer-grade. Although this breakdown has been consistent through time, the whole market is growing exponentially.

[4]   Another estimate breaks down the market thusly:
  • 70 percent individuals or small groups
  • 20 percent criminal organizations
  • 5 percent cyberterrorists
  • 4 percent state-sponsored players
  • 1 percent hacktivists ("pseudo cyberarmies," not Anonymous)

groups of individuals) can combine many different skill sets to accomplish bigger goals with bigger returns. Thus, there has been a tendency for these organizations to grow, as individuals coalesce into bigger groups over time, albeit with exceptions.

Participants

Consistent with traditional economies, the underground market comprises sellers (supply), buyers (demand), and intermediaries (Ramzan, 2013). Buyers take many forms: individuals, criminal organizations, commercial vendors. Intermediaries can act as a third party to verify and validate both products and participants; they can facilitate transactions and safeguard identities by acting as a middleman or a fence. Participants also occupy different levels in the hierarchy of the marketplace, and those at the higher levels typically receive higher compensation. Moving up into the higher and harder-to-access tiers of the market requires extensive vetting that can hinge on personal relationships.

Within these markets, there are often hierarchies and specialized roles: *administrators* sit at the top, followed by *subject-matter experts* who have sophisticated knowledge of particular areas (e.g., root kit creators, data traffickers, cryptanalysts, those who vet). Next are *intermediaries*, *brokers*, and *vendors*, and then the *general membership*. Each member can have a subsidiary cell of associated members.

Ultimately, there needs to be a cash-out. This is where *mules* and virtual money mule services come into play. They are the ones who use multiple ways to turn the stolen credit card or eCommerce accounts into usable money: e.g., completing wire transfers, shipping goods overseas bought with stolen funds. Mules can be witting participants (well-informed and organized operations), or unwitting (naïve individuals duped into involvement).

How well players fare depends on their role in the hierarchy, what they sell, their reputation, and their skill level. There is little consensus on which of these factors makes the biggest difference. In general, those higher up in the hierarchy (especially of the card and data rings) are the best rewarded. Similarly, the closer one is to the cash, the more money can be made. One expert noted that witting mules are the "linchpin" of the system, as they tend to be closest to turning "the take" of an attack into actual disbursements of money. Thus, participating as a mule can be lucrative.

Figure 2.1 depicts the different participant levels in the underground market, proportionally. It also shows the sophistication and skill levels, and gives examples of various roles.

No one knows (or is willing to hazard a guess) how many people participate in this market. Similarly, few want to estimate how large the market is, although the general feeling is that it is large, and one expert noted that it generates billions of dollars, at the least.

The number of people participating in the market is likely to increase because it is easier to get involved than it was ten years ago. This is due to the greater proliferation of websites, forums, and chat channels where goods can be bought and sold. An increase in the number of YouTube videos and Google guides for "how to use exploit kit X" or "where to buy credit cards" also facilitates entry into the lower tiers, especially for those who wish to be buyers. Sophistication will continue to rise: Wherever there is a necessity to exploit data (whether it be financial, IP, or something else) there will be highly skilled individuals selling their services. As a result, it is believed that the number of participants, particularly highly skilled ones, has risen sharply

Figure 2.1
Different Levels of Participants in the Underground Market

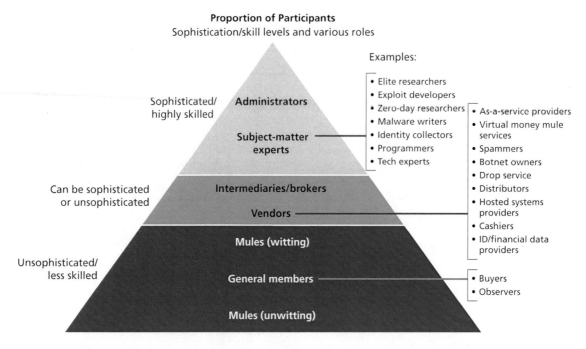

Proportion of Participants
Sophistication/skill levels and various roles

SOURCES: Drawn from interviews; Schipka, 2007; Panda Security, 2011; Fortinet, 2012; BullGuard, undated.
NOTE: Almost any participant can be a ripper; see text for discussion.
RAND RR610-2.1

in recent years, along with the variety of services offered. The level of difficulty and skill also depends on the target: In general, consumers are an easier target than organizations.

As is the case in any market, success for sellers often requires differentiating their product from others. Those who wish to sell hard-to-get, nonfungible goods often require that transactions be done in secrecy, with "double blind" auctions and the use of multiple layers to evade law enforcement.

Although there is a lower barrier to entry for the easier-to-access tiers, getting to the top tier and involved in high-level, sophisticated crimes still requires personal connections and a good reputation, especially for being trustworthy. In the words of an expert who has spent a considerable amount of time in the digital underground, "once you are able to establish yourself, it can be lucrative." Additionally, it can be a badge of honor to survive a purge.

Participants in black markets come from all over the world. Originally, key participants in such markets were former state employees of Eastern European countries who had training and education but were out of work when the Berlin Wall fell (Glenny, 2013). Since then, the sophistication of participants in the black market has soared with the entry of a generation of "digital natives" who have grown up more skilled and can do more things for themselves (i.e., they do not have to hire someone else to reverse-engineer programs or to create an exploit).

In terms of quantity, the leaders in malware attacks are China, Latin America, and Eastern Europe; Russia leads in terms of quality (de Carbonnel, 2013). Different groups operate in distinct spaces. For example, there are Vietnamese groups that mainly focus on eCommerce, whereas a majority of Russians, Romanians, Lithuanians, Ukrainians, and other Eastern Europeans mainly focus on attacking financial institutions. Chinese hackers are believed to focus more on IP.[5] Recently, some groups have partnered across international lines; one expert commented that, "groups that would traditionally never work together are working together."[6] Of late, there has been a migration toward U.S.-based actors becoming more involved; in 2013, almost a fifth of the market was made up of U.S. participants.[7] Many U.S. participants are thought to be involved in financial crime (rather than IP theft).

Business Conduits

Markets must have channels to communicate and conduct business transactions. Not surprisingly, the channels for cybercrime transactions are virtual ones. Channels initially were largely a combination of bulletin-board-style web forums, email, and instant-messaging platforms that support both private messaging or open chat rooms (e.g., some common types include Internet Relay Chat [IRC] Protocol, ICQ, Jabber, and QQ), and email. While these channels are still used today, today's participants also commonly frequent online stores where buyers can chose their desired product, pay with digital currency, and receive the goods without any interaction or negotiation with the seller. This move to mirror legitimate eCommerce storefronts indicates a growing maturity of how business is conducted. It is widely agreed that actors have gotten more sophisticated and innovative in the last four to five years regarding how they interact within these channels—making them more anonymous, encrypted, and hidden. For instance, ICQ chats have been replaced by participants hosting their own servers, sharing email accounts where content is exchanged by saving draft messages, and using off-the-record messaging, the encryption scheme GNU Privacy Guard (GPG), private Twitter accounts, and anonymizing networks such as Tor, Invisible Internet Project (I2P), and Freenet.

Participants frequently alter their communication tactics hoping to stymie law enforcement. More sophisticated participants tend to use cutting-edge tools and technologies more than others. Normally, though, they follow trends. Tor, for example, is a trend, albeit an older one.[8]

Opinions vary on where most transactions take place (it varies with product, participant, or marketplace) as well as where the most valuable interactions take place.[9] Some channels are easy to find; others are by invitation and only accessible after a great deal of vetting. In some forums, members can receive more access and privileges through participating in discussions or contributing tutorials (Paget, 2010). The forums host advertisements, but actual transactions generally take place using encrypted and private messaging, locked-down social media

---

[5]   Note that many other countries are included in the black market; only a few are mentioned here.

[6]   For example, one Vietnamese group partnered with Nigerians on a fraud scheme involving stolen eCommerce accounts. In another case, Colombians set up money-laundering "villages" in China.

[7]   In the 2006–2007 timeframe, the majority of participants were from Russia, with the United States only a small representation. In 2013, almost a fifth of the market was U.S.-based, ranked third behind Ukraine and Romania.

[8]   Here is one case where, in our interview, an expert did not want to describe a newer trend, for fear of tipping the hand of security vendors or law enforcement investigations.

[9]   Some see forums "like a Craigslist—no one knows anything; it is just a bunch of idiots talking," where goods that exist in the forums are those that have already been harvested and are just the leftovers. Others say the tools are available in the more restricted, highly vetted forums, whereas data are more publicly available.

accounts, or shared email. The evolution of accessing and interacting with the channels has been dictated by available technology. Before the appearance of the iPhone, there was very little proliferation of mobile platforms and devices with which communications and transactions could be completed anywhere, anytime. The progression of communications tools has grown with the proliferation of technology, and it will continue to be this way.

Channels and tiers are correlated. The black market has several tiers of access, with the higher tiers requiring lots of vetting before they can be entered, or even revealed. Conversely, the lowest tier (often the IRC channels) are considered easy to find, as many are publicly available and open to anyone; rippers (i.e., fraudsters) tend to frequent them, for instance. Markets in the next tier up (considered lower-tier forums) are a little harder to find and often require vetting before entry.[10] Some exclusive forums start as smaller groups where people can cut their teeth and work their way up into the bigger ones. Often, this lower tier exists in such channels as ICQ, Jabber, QQ, et al.[11] The tiers that require less vetting tend to have more financial and counterfeit goods available than sophisticated malware or exploit kits, which are found in upper tiers.

Because the black market is meant to be hidden, it is difficult to get an estimate for the breakdown of market by tier. One expert puts 10–20 percent of the participants in the highly vetted tiers, and 80–90 percent in the lower, easier-to-find tiers. Of all these players in all of the tiers, an estimate is that only a quarter can be considered highly skilled. Others maintain that there are too many variables—freelancers versus organized groups, varying types of threat actors, etc.—to make a reasonable breakdown.

Figure 2.2 shows a rough estimation of the various communications and transaction channels used by participants, for each access tier. Note that these are relative numbers and only estimates.

Language

Although English is the universal language of commerce, it is not necessarily the universal language of this commerce. Some say very little is done in English; sometimes there are English translations to supplement Russian posts, but the forums are generally in Russian or Ukrainian. There are reports of English-only, Mandarin-only, German-only, and Vietnamese-only sites, among others. Nevertheless, phishing, spear-phishing, and other social engineer campaigns are typically done in English, as a majority of potential victims know that language.

Products

The product slate is quite diverse. Products include both goods (hacking tools, digital assets) and services (as-a-service hacking, digital asset handling). Hacking goods consist of tools that help gain initial access on a target, parts and features to package within a payload, and payloads to have an intended effect on a target. Hacking services consist of enabling services to help scale or deliver a payload, and full-service capabilities that can provide a full-attack lifecycle. There are other goods and services that provide support and ensure the hacking

---

[10] Some differentiate IRC from next-tier channels, but not all. Take, for example, Herley and Florêncio (2009a) and Fossi et al. (2008).

[11] For example, Fossi et al. (2008), and Gu (2013).

Figure 2.2
Estimate of Various Channels and Tiers Used by Participants

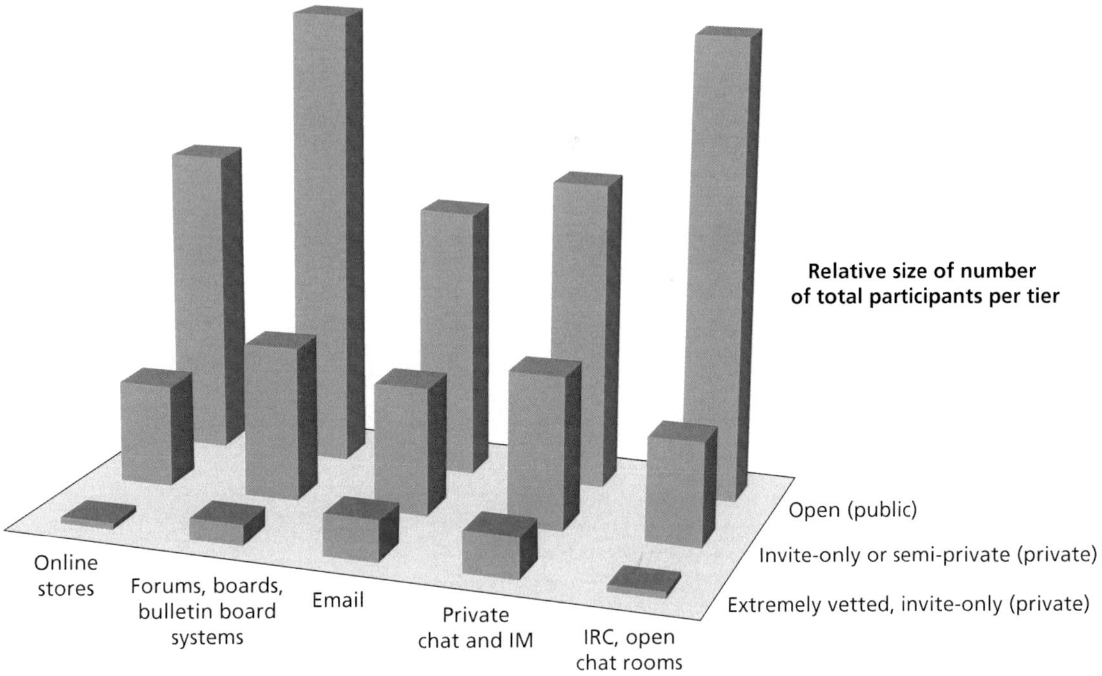

Relative size of number
of total participants per tier

Open (public)

Invite-only or semi-private (private)

Extremely vetted, invite-only (private)

Online
stores
Forums, boards,
bulletin board
systems
Email
Private
chat and IM
IRC, open
chat rooms

RAND *RR610-2.2*

goods and services function properly and are free from obstacles. These include infrastructure and cryptanalytic services, among others. Digital assets are the output from the successful hacking or hacking services (e.g., financial information, data records, accounts, IP). Digital asset–dealing includes cyberlaundering and facilitating the turning of stolen goods into money.

Table 2.1 describes the main categories of products available.

Although as-a-service offerings have been around for a while, they continue to grow in popularity as new products and technologies burgeon. For instance in 2004, as-a-service models were mainly used for adware and spyware when affiliate business models were coming into play. By 2008–2009, DDoS as-a-service became popular. The market demands more specialized, user-friendly, as-a-service models with easy-to-use interfaces, allowing more participants, regardless of technical ability, to enter the market and get involved—they simply pay for installation and have a service do the work.

Goods and service offerings are becoming much more creative (often cited as a result of the increase of tech-savvy digital natives who participate), limited only by the requirement that buyers for such offerings exist. Products have also become quieter and stealthier. Popular spyware and adware circa 2004, for instance, generated plenty of revenue, but were noisy, and garnered a lot of attention from the security industry. 2009 saw a rise in fake antivirus software, fraudware, and fakeware to steal data and credentials from machines.

Vendors often guarantee their products' lifespan or value—for example, guaranteeing a particular malware variant is good for ten hours before detection by antivirus products, or that a credit card is good for a certain amount of money—and some can track what a customer does with their product to make sure "terms of use" are not broken—a sort of "digital rights

Table 2.1
Goods and Services on the Black Market

Category	Definition	Examples
Initial Access Tools	Enable a user to perform arbitrary operations on a machine, then deliver payloads; can automate the exploitation of client-side vulnerabilities (Zeltser, 2010)	• Exploit kit (hosted or as-a-service) • Zero-day vulnerabilities (and weaponized exploits)
Payload Parts and Features	Goods and/or services that create, package, or enhance payloads to gain a foothold into a system	• Packers • Crypters • Binders • Obfuscation / evasion
Payloads	Imparts malicious behavior, including destruction, denial, degradation, deception, disruption, or data exfiltration	• Botnet for sale
Enabling Services	Assist a user in finding targets or driving targets to a desired destination to use an initial access tool and/or payload; attack vectors and scaling methods	• Search engine optimization services • Spam services • Pay-per-install and affiliates • Phishing and spear-phishing services • Services to drive / find traffic • Fake website design and development
Full Services (as-a-service)	Package together initial access tools, payloads, and payload parts and features to conduct attacks on a customer's behalf; can provide the full attack lifecycle	• Hackers for hire • Botnets for rent • Doxing • DDoS as a service
Enabling and Operations Support Products	Ensure that initial access tools and hacking services (enabling or full-service) will work as needed, are set up correctly, and can overcome "speed bumps" or obstacles	• Infrastructure (e.g., leasing services, virtual private network [VPN] services, bulletproof hosting, compromised sites and hosts) • Cryptanalytic services (e.g., password cracking, password hash cracking) • CAPTCHA breaking
Digital Assets	Digital assets are those items obtained from the target or victim (i.e., the hacked or stolen information)	• Credit card information (e.g., fullz, dumps, card verification value) • Account information (e.g., eCommerce, social media, banking) • Email login and passwords • Online payment service accounts • Credentials • PII/protected health information (PHI)
Digital Asset Commerce and Cyber Laundering	Digital asset commerce and cyber laundering, where appropriate, facilitate turning digital assets into cash	• Mule Services • Counterfeit goods and services (e.g., fake documents, identification, currency) • Card cloners, fake ATMs • Credit card processor services • Forwarding products services

management."[12] For example, a vendor might label and track each install sold, with the ability to shut down anyone who is making too much noise by infecting too many victim machines.

Malware for mobile devices has been growing of late, in part because attacking mobile devices brings in money faster than attacking personal computers. SMS (Short Message Service) Trojans and Fake Installers are the most popular form of mobile malware: They accounted for more than 70 percent of mobile malware as of March 2013, up from 56 percent in 2011 (Juniper, 2013). Such malware does not require extensive customization.

Some see a shift from opportunistic attacks to targeted attacks, and an increase in non-fungible goods (source code, IP, specific target data or credentials, etc.), while others maintain that opportunistic attacks will continue to be strong.

Finally, business models and financial innovation have grown more sophisticated. For instance, buyers can purchase stripped-down versions of a particular software or tool, or get access to goods for free; if they are happy with the product, they can pay more and upgrade to full versions—called "freemium pricing."

Pricing

The black market can be more profitable than the illegal drug trade: Links to end-users are more direct, and because worldwide distribution is accomplished electronically, the requirements are negligible. This is because a majority of players, goods, and services are online-based and can be accessed, harnessed, or controlled remotely, instantaneously. "Shipping" digital goods may only require an email or download, or a username and password to a locked site. This enables greater profitability.

According to experts, black markets operate the same ways traditional markets do. Easily exchanged goods, such as PII or account data, are prey to the normal microeconomic fluctuations of supply and demand. Often, there is too much of that product available to sell at normal prices. By contrast, stolen-to-order, nonfungible goods—such as new technology designs, details on R&D activities, mergers and acquisitions—can command a very high price, provided that the right buyer exists.

The yield of a product influences its price. A Twitter account costs more to purchase than a stolen credit card because the former's account credentials potentially have a greater yield. Immediately after a large breach, freshly acquired credit cards command a higher price— as there is greater possibility for the credit cards to still be active. But after time, prices fall because the market becomes flooded— e.g., the Target case (Kirk, 2014)— leveling off as the data becomes stale, or if there has been significant time since the last breach. This cycle continues with each new large breach. Access to botnets and DDoS capabilities are cheaper because there are so many more options (same for exploit kits). The price of PII/PHI is falling (although some believe that its value is rising).[13]

Although transactions can be done by means of nondigital currency, sites are moving toward accepting only digital cryptocurrencies, with anonymity and other security character-

---

[12] For instance, different installs of a product can be tracked to ensure a user is not getting more than what they paid for. For example, if a buyer purchases a package to infect 1,000 machines, but figures out a way to infect 10,000 machines, the supplier will cut the user off or demand payment for the extra infections.

[13] One example is Clarke (2013a).

istics. Various versions of digital currency and digital currency platforms have been around since the early 2000s. Popular ones have been Liberty Reserve (until taken down in May 2013), WebMoney, and Bitcoin. Others include Pecunix, AlertPay, PPcoin, Litecoin, Feathercoin, and Bitcoin extensions, such as Zerocoin. There is no consensus on which form of digital currency, if any, might be a clear leader; many digital currencies are interchangeable. Whichever currency prevails is likely to be chosen for its anonymity, security, and nontraceability.

Exchanges surrounding these cryptocurrencies are increasing in popularity, as are attacks on them. Experts predict that we will soon see more cryptocurrency targeting, DDoS services against cryptocurrencies, and more malware with the sole purpose of targeting wallets and bitcoins.

It is difficult to assess trends for different products; product/price relationships can be quite nuanced and depend on a variety of factors (e.g., brand name, quality of services, renting vs. buying). Although prices range widely—for example, hacking into accounts can cost anywhere from $16 to more than $325, depending on the account type (Goncharov, 2012)—similar products tend to go for similar amounts. Exploit kit prices vary based on whether they are purchased outright or rented for intervals of varied length,[14] what exploits are included, and the quality of services and products offered rather than the quantity of exploits bundled together. Brand-name recognition also plays a role. Services can involve leasing servers, finding traffic, creating a personalized payload (or "cleaning"/obfuscating an already existing payload to avoid antivirus signatures) and setting up infrastructure. See Table 2.2 for (nonexhaustive) examples of prices for exploit kits from 2006–2013, and Table 2.3 and Figure 2.3 for availability of exploit kits. Note these are just a handful of exploit kits that have been available.[15]

Table 2.3 and Figure 2.3 show the number of new exploit kits through 2013. A more concerted effort for trade activity and competition accounts for the 2009 jump. 2012 saw more "interesting" vulnerabilities found and reported—causing an increase in competitors and exploit kits, especially those from Asia (Paget, 2010a).

The cost for data records or credit cards also varies. Account records are more valuable—and hence, more expensive—if more value can be charged against such accounts,[16] they are "newer" to the market (i.e., the account has not yet been closed down by the bank or eCommerce site), or they are rare.[17] After a large breach—for example, the 2005–2006 TJ Maxx/TJX hack, the 2007–2008 Heartland Payment Systems breach, or the recent 2013 Target breach (InformationisBeautiful, undated)—the market may be flooded with data, causing prices to go down; one expert cited a price drop from $15–20/record to $0.75/record over a relatively short period. Prices for credit card data may start at $20–$45/record if supply is limited or the

---

[14] E.g., renting for a year versus renting for three months.

[15] While they are too numerous to name here, a few notable exploit kits have included: El Fiesta, ICEPack, MPack, GPack, WebAttacker, Fragus, YesExploit, Siberia, Neosploit, MyPolySploit, XCore, UniquePack, LuckySploit, SPack, Liberty, Fiesta, Eleonore, MyLoader, SEO Toolkit, JustExploit Elite Loader, Clean Pack, Shamans Dream, Max Toolkit, CrimePack, FSPack, Sploit25, MultiExploits, Tornado, Limbo, Lucky, Neon, Nuke, Spack, Sploit, Unique, ZoPack, Styx, Neutrino, Magnitude, Sakura, LightsOut, RedKit, Kore, GongDa, et al. More information on several of these exploit kits is available in Parkour (2014).

[16] For example, a credit card with a lower limit, or a low balance in an eCommerce account (e.g., PayPal) is cheaper than the higher-limit signature, gold, or platinum card.

[17] There is not always a steady supply of all types of credit cards. It can depend on where point-of-sale and endpoint terminals (like cash registers) are found to be vulnerable. For example, it may be possible to break into a terminal in Pennsylvania during a time when nothing vulnerable can be found in Germany.

Table 2.2
Exploit Kit Prices Over Time

Exploit Kit	Price	Year
Mpack	$1,000	2006
WebAttacker (Do-it-yourself kit)	$15–20	2006
IcePack	$30–400	2007
Mpack	$700	2007
Eleonore (v1.2)	$700 plus $50 for encrypter	2009
Eleonore (v1.2)	$1,500 fully managed by user	2009
Phoenix	$400	2009
Blackhole (v1.0.0)	$700/three months or $1500/year	2010
CrimePack	$400/license	2010
Eleonore (v1.3.2)	$1,200	2010
Eleonore (v1.6 and v1.6.2)	$2,000	2010
Fragus	$800	2010
LuckySploit	$1,000	2010
Yes Exploit (abuse-immunity)	$1,150	2010
Yes Exploit (Standard Edition)	$900	2010
Phoenix (v2.3)	$2,200	2010
Nuclear	$900	2010
Katrin	$25/day	2011
Robopak	$150/week or $500/month	2011
Blackhole (v1.1.0)	$1,500	2011
Blackhole (v1.2.1)	$700/three months or $1,500/year	2011
Bleeding Life (v3.0)	$1,000	2011
Phoenix (v3.0)	$2,200/single domain	2011
Phoenix (v3.0)	$2,700/multi-threaded domain	2011
Eleonore (v1.6.3a)	$2,000	2011
Eleonore (v1.6.4)	$2,000	2011
Eleonore (v1.6.2)	$2,500-$3,000	2012
Phoenix (v2.3.12)	$2,200 / domain	2012
Styx sploit pack rental	$3,000 / month	2012
Exploit kits that employ botnets	up to $10,000	2012
CritXPack	$400/week	2012
Phoenix (v3.1.15)	$1,000-$1,500	2012
NucSoft	$1,500	2012
Blackhole—hosting (+ crypter + payload + sourcecode)	$200/week or $500/month	2013
Whitehole	$200–$1,800 rent	2013
Blackhole—license	$700/three months or $1,500/year	2013
Cool (+ crypter + payload)	$10,000/month	2013
Gpack	$1,000–$2,000	2013
Mmpack	$1,000–$2,000	2013
Icepack	$1,000–$2,000	2013
Eleonore	$1,000–$2,000	2013
Sweet Orange	$450/week or $1,800/month	2013
Whitehole	$200–600/week or $600–1,800/month, depending on traffic	2013

SOURCES: Clarke, 2013a; Fossi et al., 2011; Fortinet, 2012; Goncharov, 2012; Kafeine, 2013a; Krebs, 2013a; M86 Security Labs, 2010; Martinez, 2007; McAfee Labs, 2011; O'Harrow, 2012; Paget, 2010b, 2012; Parkour, 2014.

Table 2.3
Proliferation and Variety of Exploit Kits Over Time
(non-cumulative)

Year	Number of New Exploit Kits	New Versions of Exploit Kits
≤ 2005	—	—
2006	1	1
2007	2	2
2008	1	1
2009	11	13
2010	13	20
2011	16	24
2012	28	38
2013	33	42

SOURCE: Data drawn from Paget, 2010b, 2012; Parkour, 2014; as well
as interviews with Paget and Parkour.

cards are freshly acquired, or $10–$12 if there is an influx. Credit cards acquired in the Target
breach initially fetched anywhere from $20–$135, depending on the type of card, expiration,
and limit (Krebs, 2013h). Experts note that high or no-limit cards (e.g., the American Express
Black card), or cards with chip and personal identification number (PIN) are more valuable,
and can command a higher price, and when the data begin to get stale, it may be "on clear-

Figure 2.3
Proliferation and Variety of Exploit Kits Over Time (non-cumulative)

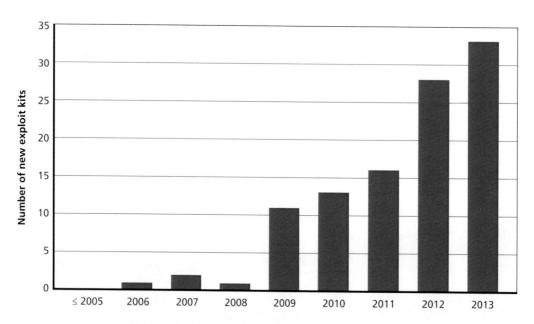

SOURCE: Data drawn from Paget, 2010b, 2012; Parkour, 2014; as well as interviews with Paget and Parkour.
RAND RR610-2.3

Table 2.4
Credit Card Prices Based on Market Circumstance

Credit Card Price	Market Circumstance
$20–$45	Freshly acquired
$10–$12	Flooded
$2–$7	Clearance ("stale" data)

SOURCE: Data drawn from interviews; Krebs, 2013g

ance" for something like $2–$7/record (see Table 2.4). eCommerce accounts (e.g., PayPal or Amazon) can be sold for a fixed price, or based on the percentage of the remaining balance.

Stolen credit card data from Europe and the United Kingdom are more valuable than data from U.S. cards for several reasons:[18]

- There is typically a delay when a card is processed in a foreign bank, so more can be charged before the bank figures it out.
- European cards often have higher credit limits.
- Many European cards (with their chip and PIN with signature system) are normally thought to be more secure that their U.S. counterparts (signature only) and are correspondingly more valuable if they can be broken and put on the black market.

IP is harder to put a value on because it can be so unique, and generally requires a specific buyer. IP can be inadvertently acquired as a byproduct of an intended goal, or can be specifically sought. There are those in the market who sell services to go after IP for a specific buyer, and those who advertise IP as a secondary gain, and who may struggle to find the appropriate buyer.

Reliability and Integrity

The black market continues to put great stock in reputation, at least within the harder-to-access tiers. Thanks to an increase in takedowns (of sites, groups, tools, or individuals), participants have labored to loosen the correlation between virtual identities and real identities. Thus, markets have seen more anonymous currencies and encrypted and stealthy communications. More of the market is hosted on darknets and through VPN services. While this trend does not affect reliability of products (some say it will make it stronger because only the highly vetted make it in), it reduces the accessibility and availability of the market. It also leads to much more intense personal vetting.

The validation of person, product, and payment can all be tricky in underground markets. Buyers and sellers validate each other through reputation, personal relationships, middlemen, or intermediaries (e.g., forum administrators). Sellers may provide demo versions or a sample of their goods. While it is a black market and thus harder to validate payment, it is also

---

[18] They are followed by countries like Australia, Singapore, and Middle Eastern countries; experts note that most Eastern European or African cards are not considered to be of much value.

a relatively small community—at least in the highly vetted, more elite tiers—where bad apples (e.g., rippers) are more quickly detected.[19]

Vetting entails either having credentials and getting vouched for by members in good standing, or proving oneself (e.g., by getting good reviews on a product presented for examination). Being vetted into the most elite tiers offers great rewards. Those accepted have access to everything they might need. Much of this vetting is based on preexisting cultures, communities, and connections. But the vetting process moves at a deliberate pace; people are particularly wary of those who promise products or services that sound too good to be true. Some members know each other on a personal level, having interacted in gaming forums or even in person; they often speak the same language (see, e.g., Qing, 2011). Some experts say such markets exist in private (e.g., ICQ-type) chat channels; others maintain they exist only in forums; still others say they exist in both, with advertising done in forums but actual transactions conducted via instant messaging. And channels may be open for less than a day to conduct business before administrators tear them down.

Vetting was rare in the early days; it was easy enough for an actor to just want to get involved, and be included. Today, vetting is more robust,[20] and the cost to entry is higher, as takedowns increase and as law enforcement and security companies get more successful at infiltrating the black market. This trend is typical of any move-countermove relationship between offense and defense. More aggressive vetting, especially for access to the high-quality sites and tiers, will mean less accessibility for newcomers, who may be viewed as suspicious. Transactions in the darknet will likely increase, which means it will be harder to get involved if one is not already, and harder for law enforcement to find these marketplaces.

Product and brand reliability also remain important.[21] As a general rule, products and services sold in black markets reliably do what they purport to do. The problem of product *integrity* comes when those reliable goods have additional unwanted "features" (e.g., a backdoor for exploit kit creators to access later). These types of features tend to show up in the lower-tier markets. Thus, performing due diligence on a product, vendor, or service is important; this may require buyers to find a due diligence service or to be tech-savvy enough to investigate matters themselves.

Because contracts in black markets cannot be legally enforced, they are constantly plagued by *rippers*, who do not provide the goods or services they advertise, and are an exception to product reliability. Rippers tend to get reported and then often quickly removed. Although

---

[19] There is some disagreement on how rampant scams are—but it mostly has to do with which markets and tiers are being discussed:
- Herley and Florêncio (2009b) focus on the lowest market tiers (IRC channels) and states that there are lots of rippers in this market, making it a lemon market. (See also Fisher, 2009.)
- One expert we interviewed stated that the markets that anyone can easily find (e.g. IRC / lowest tier) are rife with a high percentage of rippers. Of the other markets, the lower tier is approximately 30 percent rippers, whereas buyers in the higher tier rarely get ripped off.
- Another expert we interviewed stated that there are very few bad people; while the networks can comprise several thousand people, they stay relatively small and tightknit because most business is reputation-based.
- A general consensus among many of the other experts interviewed stated that, "if you can be scammed, you will be scammed," wherever you might be.

[20] One expert noted that different markets for various goods (e.g. financial data, IP, exploit kits) have their own ways of vetting.

[21] Some say these elements are similar to the noncriminal world, in that there will always be some who care about branding and some who do not.

they can easily access new channels under new names, it takes time to re-establish a reputation, which inhibits cheating. One estimate suggests that about 30 percent of the sellers (at least of financial data) are rippers, and the success rate of getting money back after being ripped off is only 15–20 percent. Unsophisticated or newer buyers are most often the ones cheated. For the most part, this happens in the lower, easier-to-access, less-vetted tier, as well as the parts of the black market that deal with credit cards and financial data, where rippers are prevalent.

Sensitivity to External Events

Different pieces of the market react differently to outside events (e.g., natural disasters, revelations to Wikileaks, or releases of new operating systems). Front-page news items are often used in spear-phishing campaigns (e.g., "click this link to donate to victims of Haiti earthquake") raising the number of potential victims. Conversely, unrest in a certain part of the world can take people there out of the market (e.g., some vendors of credit card data from Egypt were less active during unrest). This can raise the price of products as the supply decreases.

Although newer operating systems and browsers tend to be more secure against attacks, their introduction does not affect black markets immediately because developers (and their kits, programs, and products) tend to focus on the plentitude of older systems with unpatched software. When the newer systems are targeted, malware developers make sure their tools are up to date with the latest releases (e.g., can get past the latest antivirus) and can affect as many users as possible.

Resilience

The black market acts much like a traditional market; profit drives people to innovate and keep pace with rapidly changing technology. As more targets (users, companies, etc.) increase their digital connections and points of presence, the market keeps pace. Whatever is new or novel for the traditional consumer—from mobile devices to cloud solutions and new social media platforms—offers new entries for attack and will thus have a counterpart exploit on the black market.

Another facet of resilience has been the black markets' ability to survive the recent increase in takedowns, which have little effect on the size or composition of the black market. As one entity goes down, another takes its place, often within days. Although suspicion and "paranoia" spike among participants, and some countermeasures are enacted (such as stronger encryption, more vetting, increased stealth, etc.), the market just hiccups and returns to normal, albeit a somewhat less accessible and less open version of normal.

Several factors explain the recent increase in takedowns:

1. **Law enforcement has gotten better over the last ten to 15 years.** Those now coming into law enforcement have grown up comfortable with technology and computers. Training in the digital world has gotten better for law enforcers all over the world, making them stronger as an entity. Overseas partnerships and cross-pollination of ideas have also improved law enforcement—although perhaps more so at the federal

level. Leadership in law enforcement, intelligence, and the Department of Defense has accorded cyber top priority and moved resources accordingly.

2. **Suspects are going after bigger targets (and thus are attracting more attention).** Since roughly 2002, attacks have shifted from opportunistic one-offs (going after whoever may be unsecure) to attacking companies. Companies, now that they understand they are targets, are more willing to work with law enforcement, and the public-private partnership has gotten better.

3. **Crimes involving digital goods are proliferating.** In 1998, few crimes involved the digital realm (in the single digits). Starting at the turn of the century (2000–2001), more crimes were digital (about half). Now, almost everything involves a digital aspect. Because so much more crime has a digital element, law enforcement has more opportunities to encounter crime in cyberspace and learn from such encounters.

But law enforcement may become a victim of its own success. More arrests and takedowns lead to more media coverage, and hackers become more aware of the opportunities provided by black markets. Further, those already in the market grow smarter as they learn from law enforcement's investigative techniques.

Additionally, the consequences of takedowns are transitory. Consider the following:

Liberty Reserve
- Takedown: May 2013[22]
- Other Currencies Used: Immediately
- Immediately thereafter, several other types of digital currencies were up and running,[23] but so far without a clear winner.[24]

Blackhole Exploit Kit (and Cool Exploit Kit)
- Author / Administrator Arrested: October 2013
- Other Exploit Kits Up and Running: Almost immediately.[25]
- The Blackhole Exploit Kit was the most popular as-a-service exploit kit from the time it launched in late 2010 to the arrest of its author (developer and maintainer). In 2012, more than half of the web threats were cited as from Blackhole (Howard, undated). While no clear winner has emerged from Blackhole's takedown, there are plenty of viable candidates.

Silk Road
- Takedown: October 2013 (the alleged chief operator, Ross Ulbricht, was arrested)[26]

---

[22] See Krebs (2013b) on the takedown.

[23] See Krebs (2013c) on different types of digital currencies.

[24] Krebs compares it to the number of peer-to-peer systems that popped up after the takedown of Napster in the 1990s.

[25] There was a quick move from Cool Exploit Kit (a more exclusive version of Blackhole Exploit Kit) to Whitehole Exploit Kit (Segura, 2013); Arrest of alleged Blackhole Exploit Kit author, Paunch, led to reduction of spam campaigns using Blackhole Exploit Kits—but other spam took its place (Manly, 2013); Magnitude Exploit Kit replaced Blackhole (Kovacs, 2013b); Neutrino, Kore, and Nuclear Pack also remain popular exploit kits (Kafeine, 2013b)

[26] The operator assumed the moniker "The Dread Pirate Roberts."

- Version 2.0 Back Up: November 2013 (under a different Dread Pirate Roberts)[27]
- The Silk Road, a marketplace mostly known for illicit drugs, also dealt in items such as stolen credit cards and other records. Silk Road 2.0 is still finding its footing.

Carder.su

- Takedown: March 2012[28]
- Other Forums in Its Place: Almost immediately
- Carder.su trafficked in credit card and other stolen financial information. Other markets such as carderplanet, carder.pro, badb.su, etc. existed before, during, and after carder.su (Krebs, 2012; Krebs, 2013d).

Vietnamese ring dealing with identity theft and stolen eCommerce accounts

- Takedown: 2012 (Leyden, 2013b)
- After the arrest of 14 masterminds of an elaborate ring involved in selling identities and eCommerce accounts (e.g., PayPal, Amazon, etc.), other (lower) members of the group stepped up to continue operations (Krebs, 2013g).

One reason takedowns only temporarily affect the black markets is that even if a tool, forum, group, or individual gets taken down, the vast majority of what is used does not get taken down, too. For example, exploit kits are not generally proprietary, and other groups can use them or build their own based on leaked or released source code. In fact, takedowns may be beneficial for the market as the removal of a popular product allows others to vie for its now available market share. The decline of Blackhole Exploit Kit is one example of this.

Perhaps another reason that takedowns have not seriously dented the market is that many countries condone hacker activity that is illegal in the United States. One Russian hacker was arrested, let out on a technicality, apologized to, and is now connected to the government. Although Russian officials may have a good idea of what is happening, as long as they can point to fraud in other parts of the world—especially in the West—they tend to let things slide (de Carbonnel, 2013). China also tends to turn a blind eye, although there are reports of cracking down on some fraudsters.

But not all countries are like that. To give a few examples, Vietnam is very helpful, and other Eastern European countries (e.g., Romania, Ukraine, Poland) can be selectively helpful (perhaps, on Ukraine's part, to retain its option to rejoin the European Union).

---

[27] See timeline in Antilop (2014).

[28] See Ritter (2012); Warner (2009); Warner (2012); and United States of America vs [redacted], (2012).

CHAPTER THREE

The Black Market and Botnets

From the mid-2000s through today, botnets have been one of the largest enablers of cyber-crime. Not surprisingly, their presence and offerings are significant on the black market. In this chapter, we provide a focused look at botnets and their role in the black market. Figure 3.1 provides an overview timeline.

Botnets started gaining ground in the market in 2003–2004, when they were used mainly for spamming. Botnets originally operated on IRC and could be taken down by shutting down the IRC server. Nevertheless, the number of botnet variants doubled between 2004 and 2005, when the source code and a graphical user interface for creating botnets became available on the black market. This availability enabled lower-skilled users to create botnets by simply pointing and clicking (McAfee Labs, 2009). By 2007, more botnets using peer-to-peer (P2P) protocols appeared, making them harder to take down because of their distributed control (McAfee Labs, 2009; Grizzard et al., 2007). Although the most common use for botnets was still spam in 2008 (Kamluk, 2008), and 80 percent of spam was sent by botnets by 2009

Figure 3.1
Botnet Timeline

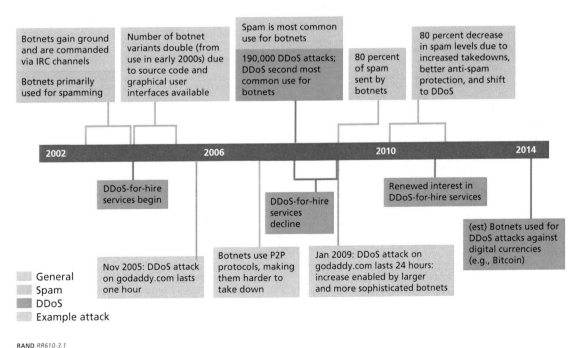

RAND RR610-3.1

21

(Namestnikov, 2009), spamming peaked in 2010 (White, 2011; Kovacs, 2013a). Spam levels sharply decreased (80 percent decrease between July 2010 and July 2011) because of a combination of takedowns, better antispam protection (e.g., by email service providers), and the shifting interest of botnet operators from spamming to DDoS attacks (Kovacs, 2013a; Symantec, 2011; Gudkova, 2013; Leyden, 2011).

DDoS attacks are another major role for botnets. In 2008, experts recorded about 190,000 DDoS attacks, and it was reported that DDoS attacks were the second most common use of botnets (behind spamming).[1] The pace of DDoS attacks has fluctuated over the past decade. DDoS-for-hire services began around 2004, but began to drop off around 2008–2009, as defenses improved. As DDoS techniques became more sophisticated, DDoS services picked up again around 2011 (just as spam levels began to decrease) and remain popular today (Leyden, 2011). Experts anticipate an emergence of DDoS attacks used against cryptocurrencies (e.g., Bitcoin), which may show up as early as 2014.[2]

Botnets have grown substantially, and that growth has greatly enabled DDoS attacks. For example, a November 2005 DDoS attack against godaddy.com lasted only one hour; just over three years later godaddy.com sustained a DDoS attack that rendered its sites unavailable for 24 hours. This second attack could not have persisted for so long without the availability of significantly larger botnets (Namestnikov, 2009). Larger botnets have also made password cracking faster and easier, allowing cybercriminals to perform tasks in hours that would have taken them years (Fortinet, 2012).

Botnets have other uses: e.g., phishing; click-fraud; harvesting credit card numbers, security credentials, and PII; providing anonymous Internet access to cybercriminals (Kamluk, 2008; Namestnikov, 2009). In the last few years, criminals have started using botnet hosts as proxies when they purchase items with fraudulent credit cards; by purchasing with an IP address from the same area as the stolen credit card, buyers evade transactional profiling by credit card companies. Mining digital currencies has become another popular role for botnets. The ZeroAccess botnet, currently one of the largest known, deals exclusively in bitcoin mining and click fraud (Symantec, 2013). Experts note that botnets can also be used to power orchestrated attacks by state-sponsored organizations.

Sophistication

Botnets have grown larger and more sophisticated over time. Early implementations were comprised of perhaps a dozen machines. Today's botnets employ millions (Namestnikov, 2009). This growth is enabled by the decentralized ability to control botnets through websites (e.g., using Hypertext Transfer Protocol rather than IRC or P2P) that exploit kits can interface with (McAfee Labs, 2009).

Botnet service models have also grown more sophisticated. Some higher-order service models sell limited-time access to botnets, or allow customers to create their own botnets based on certain targets (e.g., Bank of America accounts worth at least $10,000). Another trend many cite is the employment of dedicated purpose-built servers rented to users by seemingly legiti-

---

[1]   For number of attacks, see Namestnikov, 2009; for second-most common use of botnets, see Kamluk (2008).

[2]   For example, see Leyden (2013a).

mate "web-hosting" companies. These are much more powerful than traditional multipurpose botnet servers, because the provider can ensure that each machine is exclusively available for use by the botmaster, and not used for any other purpose.

Cost Trends Over Time

Botnet rental prices vary greatly across the large range of products available. For example, the price for a 24-hour DDoS attack in 2009 ranged from $50 to thousands of dollars, based on the size of the botnet needed to perform the attack (Namestnikov, 2009). Although many reports of botnet rentals fail to specify parameters (e.g., size of the botnet, length of attack time) and botnet characteristics vary widely, experts say that base access to botnets (especially for DDoS attacks), has gotten less expensive over time (Fortinet, 2012; Goncharov, 2012; O'Harrow, 2012; Jianwei, 2012). While a more sophisticated botnet may still carry a high price tag, botnets are cheaper in general because there is a wealth of selection available on the market.

CHAPTER FOUR

Zero-Day Vulnerabilities in the Black and Gray Markets

Zero-day vulnerabilities ("zero-day exploits", or just "zero-days") are exploitable vulnerabilities that a software vendor is not aware of and for which no patch has been created. Zero-days are thus desirable for hackers, because everyone is vulnerable to exploitation. This, combined with zero-days being difficult to find and difficult to develop an exploit for, makes them pricy. Zero-days are most often thought to be used for corporate espionage, or highly targeted attacks where the only entry is through a zero-day.

Zero-days are not as prevalent as some might advertise, but they *are* bought and sold on the black market, if one knows where to find them. What is more prevalent on the black market are "half-days" (or, as one expert calls them, "1-days" or "2-days"), where the software creator may know of the vulnerability and a patch may be available, but few users are aware and implementing those patches. For most attacks, a zero-day is not needed unless penetrating the target requires it. Generally, consumer-grade malware and tactics will get into almost any network, or "half-days" will suffice. That said, it is generally thought that if one can afford them, it is always good to have a few zero-days in one's back pocket.

Researchers have talked about the possibility of a legitimate vulnerability market (i.e., a "gray" market) for zero-days for many years.[1] Such markets now exist, but are not as well advertised or immediately accessible. Others advocate for governments and security vendors to buy zero-days actively to keep them off the black market (Gonsalves, 2013; Frei, 2013).[2]

Participants and Structure

It is difficult for buyers and sellers to find each other easily, as suspicion and the need to vet are high. Experts note that governments are increasingly showing up as buyers. Forums on this topic—e.g., bitcointalk (2013)—note several reasons why it is better to sell zero-days to security firms (or possibly governments) than on the black market—including the decreased risk of getting ripped off,[3] and the possibility of future job offers.

---

[1] Dancho Danchev (2005; 2006) proposed an eBay-like market, 0bay, back in 2005; Charlie Miller (2007) described the market. WabiSabiLabi started in 2007, with the desire to become the eBay for zero-days (Anderson, 2007; WabiSabiLabi, 2007).

[2] Additionally, there are reports that governments and security vendors are already participating this way. Advocates argue for more participation and more openness with the process.

[3] See, for example, Kumar (2013) and Pastebin.com (2013).

There is a sense of distrust about being anonymously contacted about anything related to zero-days, whether it be for purposes of information or for other means. Unsolicited approaches are not welcome; e.g., PlugBot (2013).

Because zero-days tend to be specialized for the customer, validation and verification are a must—and reputation matters a great deal, as with the other parts of the black market.[4] The fact that zero-days can be well documented helps intermediaries validate them, and validation allows people to pay serious money for them. As with the crimeware hacker market, there are third parties that broker the sale of zero-days between researchers and companies (or governments). Some third parties are themselves companies (Greenberg, 2012a, 2012b; Loidl, 2011)—e.g., VUPEN,[5] Endgame (Gray, 2011), Netragard (undated), ReVuln—but not all; e.g., bitcointalk (2013).

Prices

Little data are available on price ranges for zero-days; more is available about those on the gray market than those on the black market. However, prices vary widely depending on several factors. Zero-day prices range from a few thousand dollars to $200,000–$300,000, depending on the severity of the vulnerability, complexity of the exploit, how long the vulnerability remains undisclosed, the vendor product involved, and the buyer. Some estimates even go up to $1 million, but are often thought to be exaggerated. Zero-days' "single-use" nature also contributes to the high price (Fidler, 2014). Prices for zero-days on the black market can also fluctuate based on buyer location—that is, a buyer in Cambodia may pay less than a buyer in the United States. Prices on both the black and gray markets run much higher than the bounties that companies pay to have bugs in their own systems disclosed. Some sources say a researcher could earn 10–100 times what a software vendor with a bug bounty would pay; for example, HP's Zero Day Initiative and Verisign's iDefense Vulnerability Contributor Program only pay up to $10,000 for exploits (Critical Start, 2012; Bilge and Dumitras, 2012). As a result, some of those who offer bug bounties, such as Google, have started to increase their rewards.[6] The rise of bug bounties and increased media attention suggest a push for more responsible disclosure, along with appropriate compensation, in the white and gray realms (bugsheet, undated; NibbleSecurity, undated; bugcrowd, undated; Schneier, 2007).

Table 4.1 shows a price list for zero-days. As can be seen, data are sparse and inconsistent. While not stated specifically, it is inferred that these are gray market prices, rather than black market ones.

Some experts say the price for zero-days is decreasing significantly, and others say they are getting more expensive (along with advanced delivery mechanisms). A price drop may indicate higher volume (i.e., higher supply), or less demand (i.e., less wanted, something else has become more valuable). It appears to be more the latter; that is, the "half-days" suffice.

---

[4]   For example, it would tarnish a reputation if a zero-day was purchased and then found to be patched already, or already sold to someone else.

[5]   VUPEN claims it differs from other brokers in that it does not buy third-party products, and does all its research in-house (Schwartz, 2013).

[6]   Google's bounty program usually pays $3,000 to $5,000, with some non-Chrome exploits fetching up to $20,000 and up to $150,000 for Chrome exploits (Fisher, 2013b).

Table 4.1
Zero-Day Prices Over Time

Service	Price	Year
"Some exploits"	$200,000–$250,000	2007
"Weaponized exploit"	$20,000–$30,000	2007
A "real good" exploit	$100,000	2007
Microsoft Excel	> $1,200	2007
Mozilla	$500	2007
Vista exploit	$50,000	2007
WMF exploit	$4,000	2007
ZDI, iDefense Purchases	$2,000–$10,000	2007
Adobe Reader	$5,000–$30,000	2012
Android	$30,000–$60,000	2012
Chrome or Internet Explorer	$80,000–$200,000	2012
Firefox or Safari	$60,000–$150,000	2012
Flash or Java Browser Plug-ins	$40,000–$100,000	2012
iOS	$100,000–$250,000	2012
Mac OSX	$20,000–$50,000	2012
Microsoft Word	$50,000–$100,000	2012
Windows	$60,000–$120,000	2012

SOURCES: Greenberg, 2012b; Miller, 2007.

Trends for the Zero-Day Market

The market for zero-days (black or gray) is gaining in popularity, or at least in recognition, which may mean a potential increase in malware and attacks—one study shows that after zero-days are disclosed, the number of malware variants exploiting them increases 183–85,000 times, and the number of attacks increases 2–100,000 times (Bilge and Dumitras, 2012)—as well as security vendor and bug bounty participation. This trend could better regulate the prices, but could be negative in other aspects (i.e., drain the funds of security vendors, cause more nefarious actors to buy the more reasonably priced zero-days). Currently, there are too little data to suggest the trend in prices.

It is debatable whether there is more openness about buying and selling zero-days. There certainly is more chatter about zero-days: There are more news reports and articles;[7] companies that deal with zero-days are rising; and bug bounty programs are burgeoning.[8] But one result of this increased attention is that brokers and those who interact in this market have closed ranks and become more reticent in talking about zero-day markets. Perhaps the overall level of suspicion and due diligence have gone up. Or, perhaps, people fear losing their livelihood if

---

[7] For example, reporters Brian Krebs, Andy Greenberg, and Joseph Menn write on the topic quite a bit. Other examples include the February 2011 leaked email from HB Gary revealing that Endgame sold zero-day vulnerabilities (Gray, 2011), and Egelman et al. (2013) on the ethics and implications of the market for zero-day exploits.

[8] Bug bounties are gaining popularity: Examples include No More Free Bugs, Packet Storm, and BugCrowd, as well as vendor-specific programs like Mozilla's Bug Bounty Program. But these do not pay out the same as on the black market. So, while there is plenty more coverage and press on these avenues, a researcher can get a lot more money through other means.

they talk about what they do. One expert said the decline in openness was due to several recent reports and leaks, and a broker's clients asked him to stop talking about his work.

As awareness of zero-days has increased, access to them has not. One still needs to be sophisticated and certainly needs to know the right person (an argument for why more brokerage companies and individuals pop up to help with this) but even those "right people" stay quiet.

CHAPTER FIVE

Are Hacker Black Markets Mature?

Market maturity can be understood in several ways:

- **sophistication:** The market changes and adapts to the current needs.
- **reliability and integrity:** People and products are what they say they are, and do what they say they do.
- **accessibility:** There is a low cost of entry, and it is relatively easy to get involved, especially in the lower-access tiers—and, once vetted, in the higher-access tiers.
- **specialization:** There are distinct and customized products, places, and participant roles and division of labor.
- **resilience:** External events do not affect the market—or, if they do, the market bounces back.

Table 5.1 is our assessment of the maturity of the market. Evidence suggests that the black market is highly sophisticated and specialized, and has high continuity (resilience) as well as reliability. On the minus side, integrity is imperfect, accessibility is not predictable, and interruptions by law enforcement are increasing in the wake of numerous takedowns.

The various colors depict the general trend for each of the characteristics of maturity. Green represents a positive trend, yellow a mixed trend, and red a negative trend. In aggregate, trends indicate a growing and robust market, measured by the number of participants, volume of transactions, and amount and size of reported hacks.

Table 5.1
Characteristics of Maturity

Characteristic	Signs for (e.g.)	Signs Against (e.g.)	Overall	Trend
Sophistication	Seeing more of the "hacker concierge" concept; constant innovation in tactics and products due to move-countermove		Constant innovation to match the latest technology	Getting increasingly sophisticated; movement from ad hoc networks and groups to highly "regulated" organizations
Reliability and integrity	People guarantee a balance on a card Used to not know whether a card would work. Now, vendors guarantee the card for X amount of dollars Guarantee length of time a Trojan or malware will last before detection	Rippers can exist in all tiers. If a participant can get ripped off, they will, at any level—although the more sophisticated players and the higher-access tier participants tend to get ripped off less Extra "features" are common in products	Reliability is high, but integrity is low	Has always been pretty reliable, integrity will continue to be tested
Accessibility	"Geometric growth" of malware, exploit kits, etc., and consumer-based attacks	The best "shops" can be hard to find—need to be in the know; more suspicion of others, more vetting, more focus on anonymity	Once in, can operate freely, but getting in, especially to the high tiers, is difficult	Much more accessible and available due to proliferation of technology, but also increased vetting, movement to darknet, and use of anonymity and encryption tools
Specialization	Customized malware, as-a-service models unique to each customer		Increase in specialized roles and abilities, more customized products	Has always been pretty specialized, will continue to be this way
Resiliency	Takedowns or arrests only minimally, and temporarily, affect continuity of operations	An increase in takedowns	Despite increase in takedowns, the market bounces back (may take a little time)	The market remains continuous, even with the increase of takedowns

NOTE: Green represents a positive trend, yellow a mixed trend, and red a negative trend.

CHAPTER SIX

Projections and Predictions for the Black Market

Maturity did not come automatically or easily to the black market. It took more than a decade of continuous development and innovation, the introduction of new generations of digitally savvy participants, and significant trial and error to achieve today's maturity. Figure 6.1 is a brief synopsis of the circumstances, events, status indicators, and trends of the black market. See Appendix A for more detail.

While our experts agreed on many trends for the future, they differed on others. We first cover those that garnered consensus.

Most-Agreed-Upon Projections and Predictions

- **There will be more activity in darknets, more checking and vetting of participants, more use of cryptocurrencies, greater anonymity capabilities in malware,[1] and more attention to encryption and protecting communications and transactions.** Twitter is becoming a channel of choice; Tor and VPN services are finding increased use. Additionally, in the wake of Edward Snowden's actions with the National Security Agency, more of society is concerned with privacy and implementing encryption and protection measures, which will lead to an increase in the number of efforts to break those communications. As more data are encrypted in transit, the value of subverting machines to get to data will rise.
- **The ability to attack will likely outpace the ability to defend.** Attackers can be hedgehogs (they only need to know one attack method, but do it well) while defenders must be foxes (they need to know everything; not just technical knowledge, but knowledge of networking, software, law enforcement, psychology, etc.). Back in 2004–2005 when there was less ability to attack, the trend lines for attack and defend were close, but they have since diverged. Top-tier companies will be able to secure themselves and follow new Payment Card Industry guidelines (e.g., use of chip and PIN systems), but mom-and-pop stores will be hurt because they may not be able to keep up with these new security requirements imposed on them.
- **Black markets will require better encryption, vetting, and operational security due to the dynamic give-and-take between black-market actors and law enforcement and security vendors.** Participants will employ innovative methods and tools to help obfuscate, encrypt, or make a transaction quicker, easier to use, and harder to find.

---

[1] E.g., 64-bit ZeuS uses Tor as a communications platform (Kirk, 2014).

Figure 6.1
Black Market Timeline

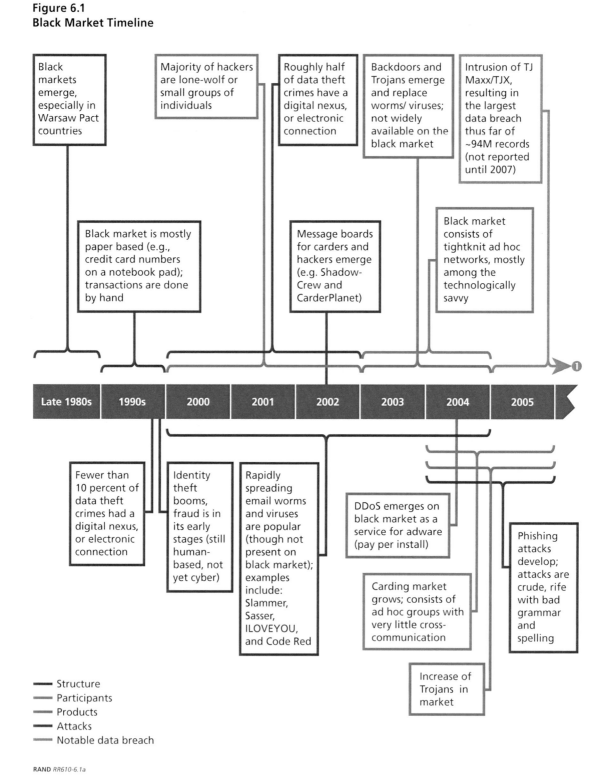

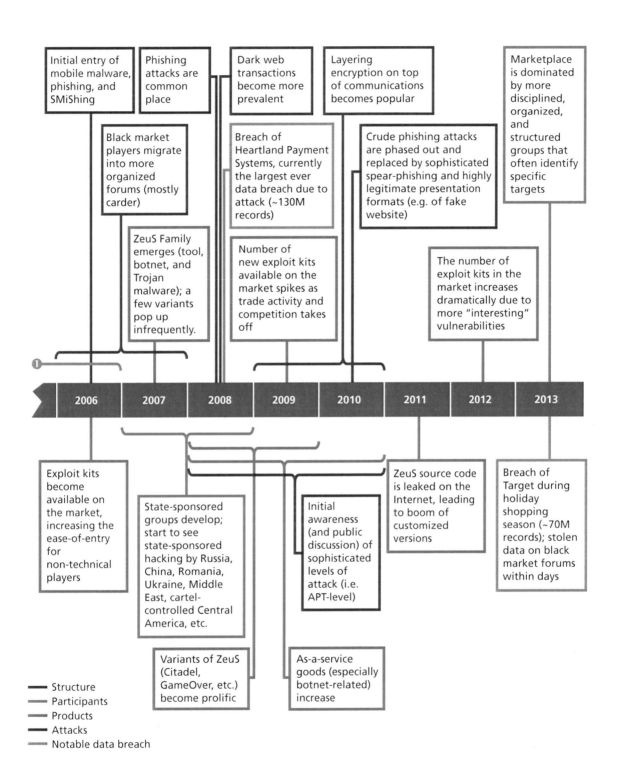

Initial entry of mobile malware, phishing, and SMiShing

Phishing attacks are common place

Dark web transactions become more prevalent

Layering encryption on top of communications becomes popular

Marketplace is dominated by more disciplined, organized, and structured groups that often identify specific targets

Black market players migrate into more organized forums (mostly carder)

Breach of Heartland Payment Systems, currently the largest ever data breach due to attack (~130M records)

Crude phishing attacks are phased out and replaced by sophisticated spear-phishing and highly legitimate presentation formats (e.g. of fake website)

ZeuS Family emerges (tool, botnet, and Trojan malware); a few variants pop up infrequently.

Number of new exploit kits available on the market spikes as trade activity and competition takes off

The number of exploit kits in the market increases dramatically due to more "interesting" vulnerabilities

2006 2007 2008 2009 2010 2011 2012 2013

Exploit kits become available on the market, increasing the ease-of-entry for non-technical players

ZeuS source code is leaked on the Internet, leading to boom of customized versions

Breach of Target during holiday shopping season (~70M records); stolen data on black market forums within days

State-sponsored groups develop; start to see state-sponsored hacking by Russia, China, Romania, Ukraine, Middle East, cartel-controlled Central America, etc.

Initial awareness (and public discussion) of sophisticated levels of attack (i.e. APT-level)

Variants of ZeuS (Citadel, GameOver, etc.) become prolific

As-a-service goods (especially botnet-related) increase

— Structure
— Participants
— Products
— Attacks
— Notable data breach

- **Crime will increasingly have a networked or cyber component; vulnerabilities will continue to persist and all agree that the human element will continue to be a weak point.** More and more interactions depend on some sort of network, digital, or computer component. Unpatched vulnerabilities (for vulnerabilities that have a patch) will remain in systems until techniques for automatic deployment of patches to users are developed and implemented. Additionally, spear-phishing campaigns will continue to grow more sophisticated.

Agreed-Upon Projections and Predictions for Shifts in Targets

- **There will be more targets, as more data become digital.** Today's organizational crown jewels are built of bytes. Back in 2003, physical security was most important to secure a company's most valuable information or goods. Today, everything is on a network—even medical records.
- **Hyperconnectivity opens up more points of presence for attack and exploitation.** By 2020, the number of connected devices will outnumber the number of connected people by a ratio of 6:1 (Evans, 2011). IPv6 will allow for people and devices to be connected, accessed, and used in a way that is impossible now (Porche et al., 2013)[2]—eventually, this may introduce better security, but initially, it enables a greater threat landscape. The Internet of Things continues to evolve; even people who might patch their computers may forget to patch everything else they own that is network-connected.
- **Exploitation of social networks and mobile devices will continue to be growth areas.** The development of mobile malware for Android devices (70 percent of all mobile attacks) is likely to continue until Google, device manufacturers, and service providers work together to find a way of delivering updates and patches to users as they come out (only 12 percent of Android devices have been updated to the versions that prevent premium SMS charges being run up on the phones of unsuspecting users).

Agreed-Upon Projections and Predictions for Shifts in Attack Characteristics

- **Attackers will continuously innovate and change tactics.** There will be more double-pronged or multistep attacks (series of attacks), with a lot more creativity and misdirection (e.g., something that looks like a DDoS, but is actually an exfiltration). There will be an increase in attacks that are made to order and that may have a long-lasting damaging effect, more ransomware and cryptlocker-type attacks that encrypt a user's personal files and demand a ransom to unlock, more polymorphic malware (which is slightly different with every installation so it can escape detection by antivirus vendors), more VM-aware malware that can evade being analyzed by malware analysts, and more stealth overall.
- **There will be a shift away from stealing credit card and financial credentials because markets are flooded with them.** The first wave of stealing data at the processor level has plateaued a bit. Once a breach has occurred, actors usually wait a little while before another

---

[2]   IPv6 is the next generation of Internet protocol—how network traffic moves.

attempt. This is to avoid flooding the market and driving down prices.[3] Experts believe that there tends to be a lapse of a few years between large breaches (e.g., TJ Maxx/TJX in 2005–2006, 94 million accounts; Heartland in 2008–2009, 130 million accounts; Target in 2013, 70 million accounts), although there will certainly still be a steady flow of breaches.

Figure 6.2 shows the biggest data breaches in history as a result of hacking (versus inside job or poor security practices).

- **There will be more hacking for hire, as-a-service offerings, and brokers.** This concept of outsourcing technical ability significantly lowers the bar for anyone wishing to get involved in the black market. Although as-a-service models will continue to grow (Glenny, 2009), there may be some changes—particularly how those providing the service store data, customer lists, and logs.[4] Figure 6.3 is one representation depicting how the growth of as-a-service models and plug-and-play interfaces has lowered the required technical knowledge of an actor to be able to implement an attack.

Agreed-Upon Projections and Predictions for Shifts in Participants

- **Digital natives will run the market, and the number of U.S.-based actors will continue to increase.** People are becoming more technically sophisticated; younger generations are using technology on a daily basis in school, learning digital technology at a very early age. In the words of one expert, "hacking has become little league: everyone starts out early, and spends a lot of time doing it."
- **Law enforcement may become a victim of its own success.** More arrests and takedowns mean more media coverage, making hackers more aware of the opportunities provided by black markets. Those already in the market grow smarter as they learn from law enforcement's investigative techniques, complicating law enforcement's job. Additionally, much of what U.S. law enforcement does, and can do, is based on older, less restrictive laws. Future laws, if developed with today's privacy concerns in mind, may restrict what U.S. law enforcement can do (e.g., how search warrants are done, how information is gathered). That said, there is an underreporting of problems, so a majority of breaches never get disclosed, a trend that may get reversed as more companies grow comfortable coming forward.
- **The best hackers are likely to leave the black market for the gray market.** Average hackers, consequently, will remain and can rise to the top of the black market.

Contested Projections and Predictions

Experts had differing viewpoints on some issues. Here are a few topics that generated disparate projections and predictions:

- **most-likely victims or targets of attack.** One expert says markets will move downscale because the larger stores can better defend themselves and have better protection mea-

---

[3] There can be the issue of too many similar goods in the market; e.g., the Target breach (Kirk, 2014).

[4] For example, with the takedown of the Blackhole Exploit Kit, customer lists and data are now in the hands of law enforcement personnel, which may make some nervous.

Figure 6.2
Hacking Data Breaches by Size

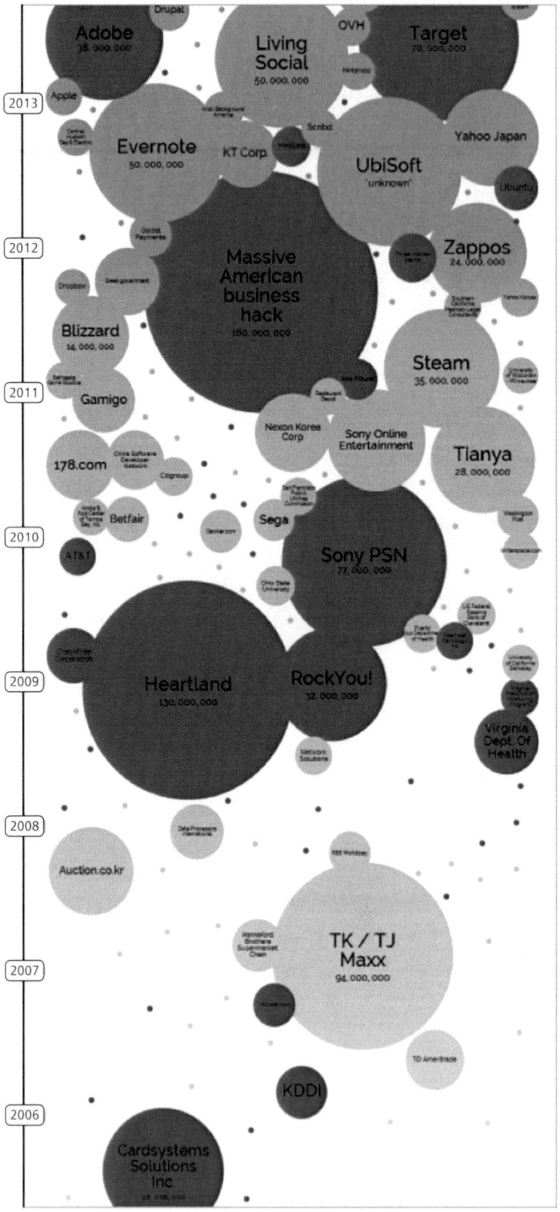

SOURCE: InformationisBeautiful, undated. Used under Creative Commons
Attribution-NonCommercial 3.0 licensing guidelines.
NOTE: The different shades of blue represent various years, and
the orange represents an "interesting story."
RAND *RR610-6.2*

Figure 6.3
Attack Sophistication versus Intruder Technical Knowledge

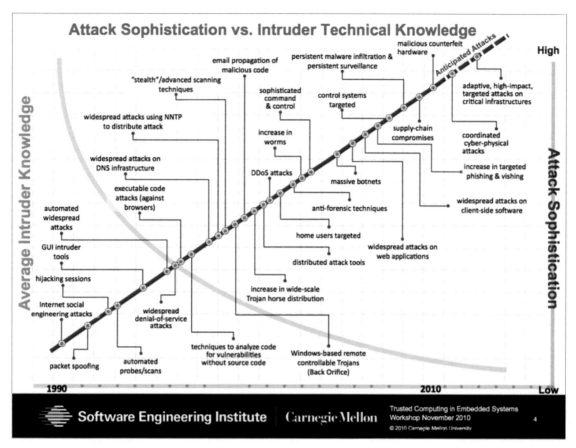

SOURCE: Image courtesy Carnegie Mellon University.
RAND *RR610-6.3*

sures. Another argues that there will be a shift to large organizations that give more of a bang for the attack buck; these are vulnerable to attack given their greater number of points of presence. Yet others say size is irrelevant; any organization with an open or vulnerable point of presence or port is a target.

- **valuing IP.** Some say attacks on IP and proprietary information are likely to rise, as state-paid hackers seek more intelligence on businesses and their financiers. Others observe that getting intellectual property (i.e., conducting espionage) requires a level of sophistication and targeted attack that very few players have, and that the take from such crimes is hard to monetize.

- **vulnerability of products that are no longer supported.** Some say the easy pickings that work against Microsoft XP are likely to dry up within two years as enterprises move to more secure platforms (e.g., Windows 7 and beyond). Others say vulnerable systems will always exist, and lower-tier hackers will continue to focus on XP and age-old attacks, even though they are not "big-dollar hacks."

- **targeted attacks versus mass attacks.** Some argue that the future will see more persistent, targeted attacks rather than opportunistic, mass "smash-and-grab" attacks. Others foresee more mass, orchestrated attacks, notably by state-sponsored hackers.

- **growth rate of the black market.** While all agree that the black market is growing, there is debate regarding the rate of growth. Some say the black market is growing geometrically because it is "stupid simple" to make malware. Others say the growth rate will mirror the growth rate of the noncriminal world and the use of new consumer technology. Still others maintain that the growth rate depends on the type of crime (financial, mass, targeted, etc.), and each type has to be considered separately. Finally, some say no baseline exists to accurately judge the rate of growth.

CHAPTER SEVEN

Conclusions

Since the mid-2000s, the hacking community has been steadily growing and maturing, as has its market. It took more than a decade of continuous development and innovation, the introduction of new generations of digitally savvy participants, and significant trial and error to achieve today's landscape. The black market does not differ all that much from a traditional market or other typical criminal enterprises; participants communicate through various channels, place their orders, and get products. Its evolution mirrors the normal evolution of a free market with both innovation and growth. The black market can be more profitable than the illegal drug trade, in that the links to end-users are more direct, and because worldwide distribution is accomplished electronically, the requirements are negligible.

As with any other market, goods and vendors in the market tend to be reliable—although bad actors do exist—and if you can get scammed (or not notice an extra "feature" in your purchase), you will be. As suspicion and "paranoia" spike because of an increase in recent takedowns, more transactions move to the darknet; stronger vetting takes place; and greater encryption, obfuscation, and anonymization techniques are employed, restricting access to the most sophisticated parts of the black market. That said, the cost to play (once in) is low because of the proliferation of as-a-service and point-and-click interfaces, and the cost to enter—at least at the most basic level—is quite reasonable because of the availability of "how-to" information. Law enforcement is getting better for a number of reasons: More individuals are technologically savvy; suspects are going after bigger targets, and thus are attracting more attention; and more crimes involve a digital component, giving law enforcement more opportunities to encounter crime in cyberspace. Yet, despite the growing rate of takedowns, the black market remains resilient and is growing at an accelerated pace, continually getting more creative and innovative as defenses get stronger, law enforcement gets more sophisticated, and new exploitable technologies and connections appear in the world. Products can be highly customized, and players tend to be extremely specialized.

The black market, once a varied landscape of discrete, ad hoc networks of individuals motivated by ego and notoriety, has now become a burgeoning powerhouse of highly organized groups, often connected with traditional crime groups (e.g., drug cartels, mafias, terrorist cells) and nation-states.

The market for zero-days is a niche aspect of the black market, and has its own place in the legitimate "gray" market.

We can expect the underground market to continue to grow and be more relevant, continue to innovate and adapt, and continue to mature.

CHAPTER EIGHT

For Future Research

The deleterious effects of black markets on cybersecurity suggest the need for options in suppressing such market activity, without which very little is likely to change. Such a search would raise several questions:

- How might bug bounty programs or better pay and incentives from legitimate companies shift transactions and talent off the illicit markets into legitimate business operations?
- What are the costs and benefits of establishing fake credit card shops, fake forums, and sites to increase the number and quality of arrests, and otherwise tarnish the reputation of black markets?
- What benefit might there be by hacking back, or including an offensive component within law enforcement that denies, degrades, or disrupts black-market business operations? Would this do more harm than good?
- How efficient or effective is it for banks or merchants to buy back their customers' stolen data (e.g., Krebs, 2013h)?
- Would implementing mandates for encryption on point-of-sale terminals, safer and stronger storage of passwords and user credentials, worldwide implementation of chip and PIN systems (already starting to happen with new standards to be in place in 2015), and regular checks of websites to prevent common vulnerabilities put a dent in the black market, or enforce significant changes to how the market operates? Would making noncompliant companies liable for data breaches decrease activity on the markets?
- What lessons learned from the black market for drugs or arms merchants could be applied to the black market for cybercrime?
- What is the best or most effective strategy for law enforcement: to go after the small number of top-tier operators (hardest to do), or the lower- or open-tier participants?
- How likely is it for governments and law enforcement worldwide to work with each other to agree to persecute and extradite when appropriate, and to coordinate for physical arrests and indictments?
- How should computer security and defense companies shift their approach to thwart attackers and attacks?

Text of the Black Market Timeline

We include the full text of the timeline graphic below. A majority of this information was compiled from our interviews with experts:

- **Late 1980s–early 1990s:** People start getting involved in the black market, especially in former Warsaw Pact countries blessed with plenty of good programmers and mathematicians suddenly out of work. There are cases of selling corporate espionage services to steal IP, but not through the black market (Glenny, 2009).
- **1990s:** The black market is mostly paper-based (e.g., credit card numbers on a notebook pad), with transactions done by hand prior to the proliferation of computing devices.
- **Late 1990s–early 2000s:** A shift of black-market activity begins, from being mainly individuals to mainly groups—but groups of those with close personal, cultural, or community connections.
- **1996–2004:** Groups of individuals, crews (e.g. Shadowcrew, Carderplanet), and organizations start to get more organized and more sophisticated (by 2001, websites for goods look professional).
- **Late 1990s–early 2000s:** Access to computing technology becomes more prevalent; more computers on college campuses lead to younger generations more familiar with technology.
- **Late 1990s:** Fewer than 10 percent of crimes have a digital nexus, or electronic connection.
- **1999:** A boom of identity theft, as more people provide information about themselves to others (e.g. for credit cards, lines of credit, etc). Early stages of fraud (human-based, not cyber) begin.
- **2000:** The concept of valuable data grows, including more than credit card data (i.e., PII and PHI).
- **2000–2002:** A majority of hackers are lone wolves or small groups of individuals (Glenny, 2013).
- **2000–2004:** There is an explosion of rapidly spreading email worms and viruses. Initially, these are "probative," later, they start to do damage to machines. Examples include Slammer, Sasser, ILOVEYOU, and Code Red. These are written by individuals (not the black market), and largely for notoriety. At first, "attacks came with press releases," in that the author wants to be known; as they start to do damage, attacks get stealthier.
- **Early 2000s:** Roughly half of crimes have a digital nexus or electronic connection.
- **2002:** ShadowCrew and CarderPlanet message boards emerge for carders and hackers.

- **2003–2004:** Backdoors and Trojans increase; things that could actually take an action, and do something. These had been around since the mid- to late-1990s with BackOrifice (1998), but they become more popular in 2003–2004 when crime starts to be mixed in (unlike a worm/virus that just spreads on its own).
- **2003–2004:** The black market consists of tight-knit ad hoc networks, mostly among those who are technologically savvy or who have a connection to those types of people.
- **2003–2004:** Financial gain rather than notoriety becomes hackers' main motivation factor.
- **2004:** DDoS emerges as a service for adware (pay per install).
- **2004:** ShadowCrew and CarderPlanet are taken down.
- **2004–2005:** Carding market grows: Ad hoc Russian and Eastern European groups form around financial crime (credit cards), involving money mules (not electronic-based); for example, DarkMarket. Ad hoc groups are all doing their own thing, with very little communication between groups.
- **2004–2005:** Markets emerge for Trojan horses. Before, buyers needed to know someone, or were done by one person (e.g., the Melissa virus was done by one person).
- **2004–2005:** The average price per card is $1–$2.
- **2004–2005:** Phishing attacks increase.
- **2005:** Forums are quite secret and large; players need to be prudent and prove they know how to exploit a particular point-of-sale machine, in order to become part of the team.
- **2005–2006:** Four to five major sites exist for credit card fraud, with about 1,500 users per site (Chace, 2011).
- **2005–2006:** Intrusion into TJ Maxx/TJX, resulting in the largest data breach thus far of ~94M records (InformationisBeautiful, undated)—not reported until 2007.
- **2006:** Phishing attacks are "cutting edge," although crude, rife with bad grammar and spelling, and obviously false websites—by today's standards.
- **2006:** Mobile malware, phishing, and SMiShing (i.e. phishing for SMS) come on the scene (McAfee Avert Labs, 2007).
- **2006–2007:** Ad hoc groups and individuals coalesce to more organized forums (mostly carders), chatter increases about hacking and further exploiting card data, home machines, or eCommerce systems. Groups begin to break out to sell software wares, exploit kits, access to hacked infrastructure, malware for hire, and surges in botnets.
- **2006:** Exploit Kits emerge on the market (WebAttacker for $15, followed by MPack for $1,000, and ICEPack for $400 in 2007). Before the availability of exploit kits, only highly technical actors were able to create and use their own exploits. Exploit kits often had technical support included. A majority of exploit kits had Russian interfaces (Sophos, 2006; M86 Security Labs, 2010; Fossi et al., 2011).
- **2007:** Exploit kit creators begin to offer discounted or free versions in response to the distribution of pirated versions of the toolkits, but with backdoors in them for the creators to exploit (Fossi et al., 2011).
- **2007:** ZeuS Family (tool, botnet, and Trojan horse malware) emerges—one of the most popular, and "most lethal" pieces of malware. A few variants pop up from time to time; by 2010, there were more than 40,000 variants of ZeuS. Law Enforcement and Security Researchers could release to the industry what was happening with initial variants, but soon were outnumbered.

- **2007:** Unique signatures of malware exceed 130,000 in 2007, versus 54,000 in 2006 (McAfee Avert Labs, 2008).
- **2007:** Most of the fraud players and cybercriminals are linked to Russia or former Soviet states (McAfee Avert Labs, 2008).
- **2007:** Activity begins to shift to being state-sponsored, as other countries see how valuable it is to get in the game.
- **2008:** Phishing attacks are now commonplace.
- **2008:** DarkMarket website (English-language forum) is taken down—transactions and prevalence on the dark web increase.
- **2008:** Heartland Payment Systems is breached; this remains the largest data breach ever, of ~130M records (InformationisBeautiful, undated).
- **2008–2009:** There is a boom of variants of ZeuS (Citadel, GameOver, etc.). Figure A.1 depicts the growth of detected ZeuS variants. Late 2008 to early 2009 saw the highest record number (the record, in May 2009, is highlighted in red), before declining. One possibility for the uptick may be due to the global economic downturn, where suddenly jobless programmers may have ventured into the black market. The downturn may be attributed to new encryption algorithms harnessed by ZeuS creators (Tarakanov, 2010).
- **2008–2009:** State-sponsored hacking by Russia, China, Romania, Ukraine, Middle East, cartel-controlled Central America, etc., increase, sponsoring cash out of the U.S. financial system. Thus, attacks become far more devastating. The atmosphere changes to more of an employee/contractor relationship than one person managing the whole thing. Activity becomes uncontrollable from a defensive point of view.

Figure A.1
Number of New ZeuS Variants (January 2007–February 2010)

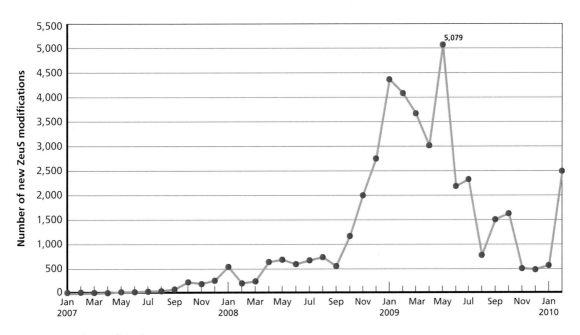

SOURCE: Tarakanov (2010).
RAND *RR610-A.1*

- **2008–2010:** The number of services (as-a-service) increases, especially related to botnets.
- **2008–2010:** Awareness (and public discussion) of sophisticated levels of attack (i.e. APT-level) increases.
- **2009:** Exploit kits' market availability spikes (Paget, 2012; Parkour, 2014).
- **2009–2010:** Use of malware to find vulnerable ports speeds up. Remote desktop protocols are used to get in. (In the past, it could take up to six months to find the weak link.)
- **2009–2010:** Layering encryption on top of communications (e.g., to evade law enforcement) rises in popularity.
- **2010:** Phishing attacks are now outmoded; sophisticated spear-phishing and highly legitimate presentation formats (e.g. fake websites) increase.
- **2011:** ZeuS source code is leaked on underground forums, causing a new boom of customized versions (Fisher, 2011).
- **2012:** The number of exploit kits in the market increases dramatically; until then, Blackhole Exploit Kit had a monopoly, responsible for 95 percent of all malicious URLs identified by researchers in the last half of 2011 (Brook, 2012).
- **2012:** Carder.su, an online forum for all things carding-related, is taken down.
- **2013:** The nominal street price is $8 per card, with mid-tier around $25 per card. For guaranteed balances, the price could be much higher (into thousands of dollars).
- **2013:** The market is dominated by more disciplined, organized, and structured groups that identify specific targets, usually companies, for their attacks (Glenny, 2013).
- **2013:** Approximately 19 percent of the market is U.S. hackers, with Ukraine and China the only two nations with higher percentages (i.e., the United States has more home-grown hackers than Russia). This may be because more organizations want to get a plant/insider within the networks. High-level executives at banks and similar institutions begin working for criminal organizations. Also, the prison systems are teaching hacking and financial crimes, so people are getting released on streets and that becomes their new set of tactics. Violent crimes go down, but financial crimes more than make up the difference.

Glossary

Adware	Software that displays advertisements, advertising banners, or pop-up ads (Cybercrime.org, undated-a).
Antivirus	Software or systems designed to prevent, detect, and remove malware, notably computer viruses.
As-a-service	Services that are delivered over the Internet or virtually, rather than provided locally or on-site (TechTarget.com, August 2010).
Attack vector	A path or means by which an attacker can gain access to a computer or network server to deliver a payload or malicious outcome. Attack vectors enable attackers to exploit system vulnerabilities (TechTarget.com, 2012).
Binders	Software used to bind or combine two or more files into one file under one name and extension. For evasion of antivirus systems (HackClarify, undated).
Black market	The trade or traffic of hacking tools, hacking services, and the fruits of hacking for malicious intent.
Botnet	A collection of compromised computers remotely controlled by a central authority. Can be used to carry out a variety of activities, including sending spam, spreading malware, launching DDoS attacks, and supporting illegal websites (Cybercrime.org, undated-b).
Botnet master	The person or persons who control(s) a botnet.
Breach	The intentional or unintentional release of secure information to an untrusted environment.
Broker	A person who functions as an intermediary between two or more parties in negotiating agreements, bargains, or the like (Wikipedia, 2014a).
Bug bounty	Reward given for finding and reporting a bug or vulnerability in a particular computer software product (Techopedia, undated-a).
Bulletproof hosting	Service provided by some domain-hosting or web-hosting firms that allow a wide range of content to be hosted.
CAPTCHA	Program that protects websites against bots by generating and grading tests that humans can pass but computer programs generally cannot. Acronym for "Completely Automated Public Turing test to tell Computers and Humans Apart" (Captcha.net, undated).

Channel (of black market)	The conduit though which participants on the black market communicate or perform transactions.
Chip and PIN	Term used to refer to credit cards with an embedded computer chip and a traditional magnetic stripe. A PIN is used to complete a purchase instead of a signature (Bank of America, undated).
Crimeware	Any form of criminal activity involving the use of computers and networks (Cybercrime.org, undated-c).
Crypter	Software that can encrypt executable (.exe) files. Crypters can be used to encrypt viruses, RATs, keyloggers, spyware, etc. to make them undetectable from antivirus systems (HackClarify, undated).
Cryptocurrencies	A digital currency that incorporates cryptography, and often has anonymity characteristics. Many cryptocurrencies are decentralized; i.e., no single institution controls the currency (CoinDesk.com, 2014; Wikipedia, 2014b).
Darknet	Anonymizing private network that uses encryption and proxies to obfuscate who is communicating with whom. Examples include Tor, I2P, freenet (Irongeek.com, undated).
Deepweb / Deepnet	Web content that is not indexed by standard search engines but can be accessed through conventional means (Wikipedia, 2014c; Dark Side of the Web, undated).
Denial of Service Attack	A type of attack used to prevent legitimate users from accessing online services or resources. Typically, a network is brought down by flooding it with traffic so legitimate traffic can not pass through (Cybercrime, undated-d).
Digital currencies	Electronically created and stored medium of exchange. Can be used like money to buy physical goods and services. Examples include Bitcoin, Pecunix, AlertPay, Litecoin, Feathercoin, Zerocoin (Wikipedia, 2014d).
Digitally based black market	The collection of (skilled and unskilled) suppliers, vendors, potential buyers, and intermediaries for goods or services surrounding digitally based crimes.
Distributed Denial of Service (DDoS) Attack	A type of DoS attack where multiple compromised systems are used to target a single system. Incoming traffic flooding a network comes from many different sources (Webopedia, undated-a).
Doxing	Technique of performing online information gathering and reconnaissance on a particular target. An abbreviation for "document tracing".
Dumps	Data stolen from the magnetic stripe on the backs of credit and debit cards (Krebs, 2013e).
eCommerce	Type of industry where the buying and selling of goods or services is conducted over electronic systems such as the Internet and other computer networks. Short for "Electronic Commerce." Examples of eCommerce accounts include: PayPal, Amazon (Wikipedia, 2014e).

Encryption	The process of encoding messages or information in such a way that only authorized parties can read it (Wikipedia, 2014e).
Exploit kit	Tool that can be used to create, distribute, and manage malware payloads, to control user web traffic, to infect users through web attacks, or to manage networks of infected machines (Howard, undated).
Fake installers	The most popular type of threat in a larger category known as SMS Trojans (Juniper Networks, 2013).
Forum (Internet)	Online discussion site where people can hold conversations, conduct transactions, or provide information in the form of posted messages. Similar to the (now mostly outmoded) bulletin board system (Vbulletin, undated).
Fraudware, fakeware	Malicious software on a computer that poses as legitimate but is really malware. It may falsely notify a user that s/he is infected with malware (PC Bits, undated).
Free market	An array of exchanges that take place in a society (Rothbard, 2008).
Freemium pricing	Pricing strategy where a good or service is provided free of charge, but money is charged for full or advanced features or functionality (de la Iglesia et al., 2009).
Fullz	Full identity information, which can include full name, email address and password, physical address, phone number, date of birth, Social Security Number, driver's license number, bank name, bank account number, bank routing number, victim employer's name (Krebs, 2011).
Fungible goods	Goods or assets that are equivalent and can be used interchangeably (*West's Encyclopedia of American Law*, 2008; Investopedia, undated).
GPG	GNU Privacy Guard, an encryption scheme.
Gray market	The exchange of vulnerabilities and exploits, the discovery and development of which are not illegal per se, but can nevertheless be troubling because they also complicate the life of system defenders.
Hactivism	Use of computers and computer networks to promote political ends, free speech, human rights, or information ethics. The use of technology hacking to effect social change (Wikipedia, 2014g).
Instant message	A type of online chat that offers real-time text transmission over the Internet. Examples of these services and programs include: IRC, ICQ, QQ, Jabber (Wikipedia, 2014h).
Intellectual property (IP)	A work or invention that is the result of creativity, such as a manuscript or a design, to which one has rights and for which one may apply for a patent, copyright, trademark, etc. (Wikipedia, 2014i).
Invisible Internet Project (I2P)	An example of a darknet. Used as an anonymizing layer to connect to other I2P websites, anonymous email, and the public Internet (Irongeek. com, undated).

Malware	Software that is intended to damage or disable computers or computer systems. Types of malware include viruses, worms, and Trojans (Wikipedia, 2014j).
Marketplace	The location in which a market operates; can be physical or virtual.
Mule	A person (or service) who transfers illegally acquired money or goods on behalf of others. Mules can be unwitting or witting participants; i.e. naïve individuals duped into involvement, or well-informed and organized operations.
Nonfungible good	Goods or assets that are not easy to exchange or mix with other similar goods or assets (Cambridge Dictionaries Online, undated).
Obfuscation	Method or tool used to make code more complicated to read while retaining functionality. It can be used to increase the security of a program, or used to bypass security features or AV detection (Techopedia, undated-b).
Off the record	Cryptographic protocol that provides strong encryption for instant message conversations (Wikipedia, 2014j).
Packers	The "outer shell" of some malware; e.g., Trojans, to hide the malware and make detection and analysis by antivirus software more difficult. Packers can also employ antidebugging, antiemulation, anti-VM techniques and code obfuscation (ES/ET Virus Radar, undated).
Payload	The component of malware that executes a malicious activity (Techopedia, undated-c).
Pay-per-install (PPI) (services and affiliates)	Specialized organizations that focus on the infection of victims' systems. They provide a means to outsource the global dissemination of malware (Caballero et al., undated).
Peer-to-peer (P2P) network	Type of decentralized and distributed network architecture in which individual nodes in the network (peers) connect to each other. Contrast with a centralized client-server model where client nodes request access to resources provided by central servers (Wikipedia, 2014k) .
Personally identifiable information (PII)	Information that can be used to distinguish or trace an individual's identity. Can include name, Social Security Number, biometric records, date and place of birth, mother's maiden name, driver's license number, financial account information (iDash, undated).
Phishing	The act of attempting to acquire information—such as usernames, passwords, and financial information—by masquerading as a trustworthy entity using electronic communications such as email (Wikipedia, 2014l).
Point-of-sale terminals	The place where a retail transaction is completed; the point at which a customer makes a payment to the merchant in exchange for goods or services (Wikipedia, 2014m).
Product	Collection of economic output, including physical goods and intangible services (Wikipedia, 2014n).

Protected health information (PHI)	Individually identifiable health information, including demographic data, that relates to an individual's past, present, or future physical mental health or condition; provision of health care to the individual; past, present, or future payment for the provision of health care to the individual (iDash, undated).
Ransomware	A class of malware that restricts access to the computer system it infects, and demands a ransom paid to the creator of the malware for the restriction to be removed (Wikipedia, 2014o).
Rippers	Participants in the underground market who do not provide the goods or services they advertise.
Search engine optimization	Process of affecting the visibility of a website or a web page in a search engine's "natural" or unpaid ("organic") search results (Wikipedia, 2014p).
SMS Trojans	A type of malware that surreptitiously sends SMS text messages to premium text messaging services (Juniper Networks, undated).
Social engineering	The act of influencing an entity (e.g., a person) to accomplish goals that may or may not be in that entity's best interest. It may include obtaining information, gaining access, or getting the entity to take certain action (Social-Engineer.org, undated).
Spam	Unsolicited, irreverent, or inappropriate messages sent on the Internet to a large number of recipients. May include malware or malicious links. Electronic junk mail (Webopedia, undated-b; Wikipedia, 2014q).
Spear-phishing	Phishing attempts directed at specific individuals or companies. Used by attackers to gather personal information about targets to increase probability of success (Wikipedia, 2014l).
Spyware	Software that covertly gathers user information (e.g., passwords, financial and account credentials) without the user's knowledge (Webpoedia, undated-c).
The Onion Router (Tor)	An example of a darknet. Used as an anonymizing layer, it directs Internet traffic through a free, worldwide, volunteer network to conceal a user's location or usage (Wikipedia, 2014r).
Tier (of black market)	Access levels for participants on the black market; how participants operate in order to perform transactions and communications.
Virtual machine	Software-based emulation of a computer (Wikipedia, 2014s) .
Virtual private network (VPN)	Extends a private network across a public network, such as the Internet. Enables a computer to send and receive data across shared or public networks as if it were directly connected to the private network, while benefiting from the functionality, security, and management policies of the private network (Wikipedia, 2014t).
Vulnerability	A software, hardware, procedural, or human weakness that may provide an attacker with an open door with which to exploit.

Watering hole attack	An attack that compromises a popular or well-trafficked website by leaving a piece of malware that will infect all legitimate users visiting the site.
Zero-day vulnerabilities	Exploitable vulnerabilities that a software vendor is not aware of and for which no patch has been created.
ZeuS	Malware (Trojan) that can be used for malicious purposes. Uses include stealing banking information and installing other malware (e.g., CryptoLocker ransomware) (Wikipedia, 2014u).

Bibliography

Allodi, Luca, and Fabio Massacci, *Some Preliminary Analysis of the Economics of Malware Kits and Traffic Brokers,* presentation delivered at the Workshop on Collaborative Security and Privacy Technologies, Berlin, Germany, April 25, 2012. As of November 2, 2013:
https://securitylab.disi.unitn.it/lib/exe/fetch.php?media=euforum2012.pdf

———, *Economics of Cybercrime,* presentation delivered at the Joint meeting with Ufa State Aviation University Russia, Trento, Italy, May 14, 2012. As of November 2, 2013:
https://securitylab.disi.unitn.it/lib/exe/fetch.php?media=ufa.pdf

Anderson, Nate, "WabiSabiLabi Wants to Be the eBay of 0-Day Exploits," arstechnica.com, July 9, 2007. As of February 4, 2014:
http://arstechnica.com/security/2007/07/wabisabilabi-wants-to-be-the-ebay-of-0-day-exploits/

Andrews, Archie, *Trusted Computing in Embedded Systems: Challenges*, Pittsburgh, Pa.: Trusted Computing in Embedded Systems Workshop, Carnegie Mellon University, November 2010.

Antilop, "Silk Road," antilop.cc, January 22, 2014. As of February 4, 2014:
http://antilop.cc/sr/

Bank of America, *Credit Card FAQs: What Is a Chip Card?* web page, undated. As of February 20, 2014:
https://www.bankofamerica.com/credit-cards/chip-and-signature-faq.go

Bilge, Leyla, and Tudor Dumitras, *Before We Knew It: An Empirical Study of Zero-Day Attacks in the Real World*, proceedings of the 2012 ACM Conference on Computer and Communications Security, ACM, 2012, pp. 833–844. As of February 4, 2014:
http://users.ece.cmu.edu/~tdumitra/public_documents/bilge12_zero_day.pdf

bitcointalk, "Where Can I Sell a 0 Day?" bitcointalk.org, September 16, 2013. As of February 4, 2014:
https://bitcointalk.org/index.php?topic=295200.5;wap

Brook, Chris, "Blackhole Exploit Kit's Dominance on Infected Hosts Could Push Rivals to the Cloud," threatpost.com, February 8, 2012. As of February 2014:
http://threatpost.com/blackhole-exploit-kits-dominance-infected-hosts-could-push-rivals-cloud-020812/76183

bugcrowd, "The Bug Bounty List," bugcrowd.com, undated. As of February 4, 2014:
https://bugcrowd.com/list-of-bug-bounty-programs/

bugsheet, "Bug Bounties and Disclosure Programs," bugsheet.com, undated. As of February 4, 2014:
http://www.bugsheet.com/bug-bounties

BullGuard, "The Online Black Market—How It Works (Part I)," bullguard.com, undated. As of February 6, 2014:
http://www.bullguard.com/bullguard-security-center/internet-security/internet-threats/online-black-market-part-i.aspx

Caballero, Juan, Chris Grier, Christian Kreibich, and Vern Paxson, *Measuring Pay-per-Install: The Commoditization of Malware Distribution*, undated. As of February 20, 2014:
https://www.usenix.org/legacy/events/sec11/tech/full_papers/Caballero.pdf

Cambridge Dictionaries Online, Nonfungible, web page, undated. As of February 20, 2014:
http://dictionary.cambridge.org/us/dictionary/business-english/nonfungible

Captcha.net, *CAPTCHA: Telling Humans and Computers Apart Automatically*, web page, undated. As of February 20, 2014:
http://www.captcha.net/

Chace, Zoe, "The FBI Agent Who Became a Black-Market Mogul," npr.org, June 17, 2011. As of February 4, 2014:
http://www.npr.org/blogs/money/2011/06/17/137251254/the-fbi-agent-who-ran-a-stolen-credit-card-ring

Christin, Nicolas, *Traveling the Silk Road: A Measurement Analysis of a Large Anonymous Online Marketplace,* Pittsburgh, Pa.: CMU CyLab, July 30, 2012.

Clarke, Elizabeth, "Hackers Sell Health Insurance Credentials, Bank Accounts, SSNs and Counterfeit Documents, for Over $1,000 per Dossier," Dell, SecureWorks.com/Security and Compliance blog, July 15, 2013a. As of February 3, 2014:
http://www.secureworks.com/resources/blog/general-hackers-sell-health-insurance-credentials-bank-accounts-ssns-and-counterfeit-documents/

———, "The Underground Hacking Economy is Alive and Well," Dell, SecureWorks.com/Security and Compliance blog, November 18, 2013b. As of February 3, 2014:
http://www.secureworks.com/resources/blog/the-underground-hacking-economy-is-alive-and-well

CoinDesk, *What Is Bitcoin?* web page, undated. As of February 20, 2014:
http://www.coindesk.com/information/what-is-bitcoin/

Critical Start, "Be a Millionaire: The Market for Zero-Day Software Exploits," criticalstart.com, April 2012. As of October 31, 2013:
http://www.criticalstart.com/2012/04/be-a-millionaire-the-market-for-zero-day-software-exploits/

Cybercrime.org, *Safety and Security Guide, Adware Definition*, web page, undated-a. As of February 20, 2014:
http://cybercrime.org.za/adware/

———, *Safety and Security Guide, Botnet Definition*, web page, undated-b. As of February 20, 2014:
http://cybercrime.org.za/botnet/

———, *Safety and Security Guide, Crimeware Definition*, web page, undated-c. As of February 20, 2014:
http://cybercrime.org.za/crimeware/

———, *Safety and Security Guide, Denial-of-Service Attack Definition*, web page, undated-d. As of February 20, 2014:
http://cybercrime.org.za/dos-attack/

Danchev, Dancho, "0bay—How Realistic Is the Market for Security Vulnerabilities?" ddanchev.blogspot.com, December 12, 2005. As of February 4, 2014:
http://ddanchev.blogspot.com/2005/12/0bay-how-realistic-is-market-for.html

———, "Where's My 0day, Please?" ddanchev.blogspot.com, March 7, 2006. As of February 4, 2014:
http://ddanchev.blogspot.com/2006/03/wheres-my-0day-please.html

Dark Side of the Web, *The Dark Web*, web page, undated. As of February 20, 2014:
http://davidenewmedia.wordpress.com/workingterms/darkweb/

de Carbonnel, Alissa, "Hackers for Hire: Ex-Soviet Tech Geeks Play Outsized Role in Global Cyber Crime," NBCNews.com/Technology, August 22, 2013. As of February 3, 2014:
http://www.nbcnews.com/technology/hackers-hire-ex-soviet-tech-geeks-play-outsized-role-global-6C10981346

de la Iglesia, Jose Luis Marín, and Jose Emilio Labra Gayo. "Doing Business by Selling Free Services," in *Web 2.0: The Business Model*, Miltiadis D. Lytras, Ernesto Damiani, Patricia Ordóñez de Pablos, (eds.), Springer eBooks, 2009.

Egelman, Serge, Cormac Herley, and Paul C. van Oorschot, *Markets for Zero-Day Exploits: Ethics and Implications*, NSPW '13, September 9, 2013. As of February 4, 2014:
http://people.scs.carleton.ca/~paulv/papers/NSPW-2013-author-version.pdf

ES/ET Virus Radar, *Packer, Crypter, Protector*, web page, undated. As of February 20, 2014:
http://www.virusradar.com/en/glossary/packer-crypter-protector

Evans, Dave, *The Internet of Things: How the Next Evolution of the Internet Is Changing Everything,* San Jose, Calif.: Cisco Systems, Inc., April 2011. As of February 3, 2014:
http://www.cisco.com/web/about/ac79/docs/innov/IoT_IBSG_0411FINAL.pdf

Farivar, Cyrus, "Ukranian Fraudster and CarderPlanet 'Don' Finally Sentenced to 18 Years," arstechnica.com, December 12, 2013. As of February 4, 2014:
http://arstechnica.com/tech-policy/2013/12/ukranian-fraudster-and-carderplanet-don-finally-sentenced-to-18-years/

Fidler, Mailyn, *Anarchy or Regulation? International Security Implications of Global Markets for Zero-Day Vulnerabilities,* honors thesis, Stanford University Center for International Security and Cooperation, forthcoming, June 2014.

Fisher, Dennis, "Cormac Herley on the Underground Economy, IRC Economics and the Externalities of Cybercrime," threatpost.com/Digital Underground podcast, June 12, 2009. As of October 30, 2013:
http://threatpost.com/tag/cormac-herley

———, "Zeus Source Code Leaked," threatpost.com blog, May 10, 2011. As of February 3, 2014:
http://threatpost.com/zeus-source-code-leaked-051011/75217

———, "Researchers Find Bug Bounty Programs Pay Economic Rewards," threatpost.com, July 10, 2013a. As of February 4, 2014:
https://threatpost.com/researchers-find-bug-bounty-programs-pay-economic-rewards/101243

———, "After Paying $2 Million in Rewards, Google Multiplies Some Bug Bounties Five Times," threatpost.com blog, August 12, 2013b. As of November 11, 2013:
http://threatpost.com/after-paying-2m-in-rewards-google-multiplies-some-bug-bounties-five-times

Finkle, Jim, and Joseph Menn, "Suspect in 'Blackhole' Cybercrime Case Arrested in Russia: Source," Reuters.com, October 13, 2013. As of November 2, 2013:
http://www.reuters.com/article/2013/10/13/net-us-cybercrime-arrest-idUSBRE99714Y20131013

Fortinet, *Cybercriminals Today Mirror Legitimate Business Processes: 2013 Cybercrime Report,* Sunnyvale, Calif.: Fortinet Inc., December 2012. As of November 11, 2013:
http://www.fortinet.com/sites/default/files/whitepapers/Cybercrime_Report.pdf

Fossi, Marc, Gerry Egan, Eric Johnson, Trevor Mack, Téo Adams, Joseph Blackbird, Brent Graveland, and David McKinney, *Symantec Report on Attack Kits and Malicious Websites,* Mountain View, Calif.: Symantec, 2011. As of February 3, 2014:
https://scm.symantec.com/resources/b-symantec_report_on_attack_kits_and_malicious_websites_21169171_WP.en-us.pdf

Fossi, Marc, Eric Johnson, Dean Turner, Trevor Mack, Joseph Blackbird, David McKinney, Mo King Low, Téo Adams, Marika Pauls Laucht, and Jesse Gough, *Symantec Report on the Underground Economy July 07–June 08,* Cupertino, Calif.: Symantec Corporation, November 2008. As of October 31, 2013:
http://eval.symantec.com/mktginfo/enterprise/white_papers/b-whitepaper_underground_economy_report_11-2008-14525717.en-us.pdf

Frei, Stefan, *The Known Unknowns,* NSS Labs, December 5, 2013. As of February 4, 2014:
https://www.nsslabs.com/reports/known-unknowns-0

Gendarmerie Nationale, *Prospective Analysis on Trends in Cybercrime from 2011 to 2020,* trans., Santa Clara, Calif.: McAfee Labs, 2011. As of February 3, 2014:
http://www.mcafee.com/us/resources/white-papers/wp-trends-in-cybercrime-2011-2020.pdf

Gjelten, Tom, "In Cyberwar, Software Flaws Are A Hot Commodity," npr.org/news, February 12, 2013. As of November 11, 2013:
http://www.npr.org/2013/02/12/171737191/in-cyberwar-software-flaws-are-a-hot-commodity

Glenny, Misha, "How Global Crime Networks Work," ted.com, July 2009. As of February 4, 2014:
http://www.ted.com/talks/misha_glenny_investigates_global_crime_networks.html

———, "Cyber Subterfuge," NYTimes.com/International Herald Tribune, November 27, 2013. As of February 3, 2014:
http://www.nytimes.com/2013/11/28/opinion/cyber-subterfuge.html?_r=2&pagewanted=all&

Goncharov, Max, *Russian Underground 101*, Cupertino, Calif.: Trend Micro Incorporated, 2012. As of November 11, 2013:
http://www.trendmicro.com/cloud-content/us/pdfs/security-intelligence/white-papers/wp-russian-underground-101.pdf

Gonsalves, Antone, "Good Guys Should Compete with Criminals in Buying Zero-Day Vulnerabilities, Report Says," csoonline.com, December 17, 2013. As of February 4, 2014:
http://www.csoonline.com/article/744802/good-guys-should-compete-with-criminals-in-buying-zero-day-vulnerabilities-report-says

Goodin, Dan, "Microsoft Defense that Fetched $50,000 Prize Bypassed in Just 2 Weeks," arstechnica.com, August 8, 2012a. As of November 11, 2013: http://arstechnica.com/security/2012/08/microsoft-defense-bypassed-in-2-weeks/

———, "Google Pledges $2 Million in Prizes to Hackers Who Exploit Chrome," arstechnica.com, August 15, 2012b. As of November 11, 2013:
http://arstechnica.com/security/2012/08/google-pledges-million-in-hacking-prizes/

———, "Google Chrome Exploit Fetches 'Pinkie Pie' $60,000 Hacking Prize," arstechnica.com, October 10, 2012c. As of November 11, 2013:
http://arstechnica.com/security/2012/10/google-chrome-exploit-fetches-pinkie-pie-60000-hacking-prize/

———, "$5,000 Will Buy You Access to Another, New Critical Java Vulnerability (Updated)," arstechnica.com, January 16, 2013. As of November 11, 2013:
http://arstechnica.com/security/2013/01/5000-will-buy-you-access-to-another-new-critical-java-vulnerability/

Gray, Patrick, "HBGary's Leaked E-Mail Ain't Getting Boring Yet," risky.biz, February 21, 2011. As of February 4, 2014:
http://risky.biz/endgame

Greenberg, Andy, "Meet The Hackers Who Sell Spies the Tools to Crack Your PC (and Get Paid Six-Figure Fees)," Forbes.com, March 21, 2012a. As of November 11, 2013:
http://www.forbes.com/sites/andygreenberg/2012/03/21/meet-the-hackers-who-sell-spies-the-tools-to-crack-your-pc-and-get-paid-six-figure-fees/

———, "Shopping For Zero-Days: A Price List for Hackers' Secret Software Exploits," Forbes.com, March 23, 2012b. As of February 3, 2014:
http://www.forbes.com/sites/andygreenberg/2012/03/23/shopping-for-zero-days-an-price-list-for-hackers-secret-software-exploits/

Grizzard, Julian B., Vikram Sharma, Chris Nunnery, Brent ByungHoon Kang, and David Dagon, "Peer-to-Peer Botnets: Overview and Case Study," In proceedings of the first conference on *First Workshop on Hot Topics in Understanding Botnets*, 2007. As of February 4, 2014:
https://www.usenix.org/legacy/events/hotbots07/tech/full_papers/grizzard/grizzard_html/

Gu, Lion, *Beyond Online Gaming Cybercrime: Revisiting the Chinese Underground Market*, Cupertino, Calif.: Trend Micro Incorporated, 2013. As of February 4, 2014:
http://www.trendmicro.com/cloud-content/us/pdfs/security-intelligence/white-papers/wp-beyond-online-gaming-cybercrime.pdf

Gudkova, Darya, "Kaspersky Security Bulletin: Spam Evolution 2012," securelist.com, January 21, 2013. As of February 4, 2014:
http://www.securelist.com/en/analysis/204792276/Kaspersky_Security_Bulletin_Spam_Evolution_2012

Guido, Dan, "A Case Study of Intelligence-Driven Defense," *IEEE Security and Privacy*, November/December 2011, pp. 67–70. As of February 3, 2014:
http://www.trailofbits.com/resources/exploit_intelligence_project_paper.pdf

HackClarify, *Hiding Keyloggers/Rats/Worms/Viruses Using Crypters or Binders*, web page, undated. As of February 20, 2014:
http://hackclarify.blogspot.com/2012/05/hiding-keyloggersratswormsviruses-using.html

Haley, Kevin, and Kat Pelak, "Full Service Hackers for Hire," *Semantec Webcast*, October 15, 2013.

Herley, Cormac, and Dinei Florêncio, *Economics and the Underground Economy*, presentation delivered at BlackHat, Washington, D.C., February 18–19, 2009a. As of February 3, 2014:
http://research.microsoft.com/en-us/um/people/cormac/papers/2009/Blackhat09.pdf

———, "Nobody Sells Gold for the Price of Silver: Dishonesty, Uncertainty and the Underground Economy," *Microsoft Research*, June 2009b. As of February 3, 2024:
http://research.microsoft.com/pubs/80034/nobodysellsgoldforthepriceofsilver.pdf

Howard, Fraser, "Exploring the Blackhole Exploit Kit," nakedsecurity.sophos.com, undated. As of February 4, 2014:
http://nakedsecurity.sophos.com/exploring-the-blackhole-exploit-kit-14/

iDash, *PHI and PII Definition and Data Elements*, web page, undated. As of February 20, 2014:
http://idash.ucsd.edu/phi-and-pii-definition-and-data-elements

InformationWeek, "NSA Contracted with Zero-Day Vendor Vupen," September 17, 2013. As of February 3, 2014:
http://www.informationweek.com/security/risk-management/
nsa-contracted-with-zero-day-vendor-vupen/d/d-id/1111564

InformationisBeautiful, "World's Biggest Data Breaches," undated. As of February 4, 2014:
http://www.informationisbeautiful.net/visualizations/worlds-biggest-data-breaches-hacks/

Infosec Institute, "The Impact of Cybercrime 2013," November 1, 2013. As of November 2, 2013:
http://resources.infosecinstitute.com/2013-impact-cybercrime/

Investopedia, *Fungibles*, web page, undated. As of February 20, 2014:
http://www.investopedia.com/terms/f/fungibles.asp

Irongeek.com, *Intro to Darknets: Tor and I2P Workshop*, web page, undated. As of February 20, 2014:
http://www.irongeek.com/i.php?page=videos/intro-to-tor-i2p-darknets

Jianwei, Zhuge, Gu Liang, and Duan Haixin, *Investigating China's Online Underground Economy*, Study of Innovation and Technology in China, the University of California Institute on Global Conflict and Cooperation, July 2012. As of November 11, 2013:
http://igcc.ucsd.edu/assets/001/503677.pdf

Joostbijl, "Malicious Advertisements Served via Yahoo," blog.fox-it.com, January 3, 2014. As of February 4, 2014:
http://blog.fox-it.com/2014/01/03/malicious-advertisements-served-via-yahoo/

Jones, Jason, *State of Web Exploit Kits*, presentation at BlackHat, Las Vegas, Nev., July 21–26, 2012. As of November 5, 2013:
https://media.blackhat.com/bh-us-12/Briefings/Jones/BH_US_12_Jones_State_Web_Exploits_Slides.pdf;

———, *State of Web Exploit Kits*, BlackHat Conference Proceedings, Las Vegas, Nev., July 21–26, 2012. As of November 5, 2013:
https://media.blackhat.com/bh-us-12/Briefings/Jones/BH_US_12_Jones_State_Web_Exploits_WP.pdf

Juniper Networks, Inc., *Juniper Networks Third Annual Mobile Threats Report*, Sunnyvale, Calif., 2013. As of February 3, 2014:
http://www.juniper.net/us/en/local/pdf/additional-resources/jnpr-2012-mobile-threats-report.pdf

Kafeine, "Briefly Wave WhiteHole Exploit Kit Hello…," Malware Don't Beed Coffee blog, February 4, 2013a. As of February 3, 2014:
http://malware.dontneedcoffee.com/2013/02/briefly-wave-whitehole-exploit-kit-hello.html

———, "Magnitude EK: Pop Pop !," Malware Don't Beed Coffee blog, October 2013b. As of February 4, 2014:
http://malware.dontneedcoffee.com/2013/10/Magnitude.html

Kamluk, Vitaly, "The Botnet Business," SecureList.com/Analysis, May 13, 2008. As of February 3, 2014:
http://www.securelist.com/en/analysis/204792003/The_botnet_business

Kassner, Michael, "Guess Who's Buying Zero-Day Vulnerabilities?" TechRepublic.com, June 18, 2012. As of November 11, 2013:
http://www.techrepublic.com/blog/it-security/guess-whos-buying-zero-day-vulnerabilities/

Keizer, Gregg, "Google Pays Record $31K Bounty for Chrome Bugs," techworld.com, April 29, 2013. As of November 11, 2013:
http://news.techworld.com/applications/3444615/google-pays-record-31k-bounty-for-chrome-bugs/

Kessler, Mike, "The Pest Who Shames Companies into Fixing Security Flaws," Wired.com, November 23, 2011. As of November 11, 2013:
http://www.wired.com/magazine/2011/11/mf_soghoian/

Kirk, Jeremy, "CloudeyeZ Tracks Underground Prices of Stolen Credit Card Data in Real-Time," NetworksAsia.net, October 11, 2013. As of November 11, 2013:
http://networksasia.net/article/cloudeyez-tracks-underground-prices-stolen-credit-card-data-real-time-1344220037

———, "Target Hackers Have More Data Than They Can Sell," infoworld.com, January 14, 2014. As of February 2014:
http://www.infoworld.com/d/security/target-hackers-have-more-data-they-can-sell-234116

Kovacs, Eduard, "Volume of Spam Decreased in 2012 Because of Anti-Spam Protection, Kaspersky Says," softpedia.com, January 21, 2013a. As of February 4, 2014:
http://news.softpedia.com/news/Volume-of-Spam-Decreased-in-2012-Because-of-Anti-Spam-Protection-Kaspersky-Says-322872.shtml

———, "Cutwail Cybercriminals Replace BlackHole with Magnitude Exploit Kit," Softpedia.com, October 22, 2013b. As of November 11, 2013:
http://news.softpedia.com/news/Cutwail-Cybercriminals-Replace-BlackHole-with-Magnitude-Exploit-Kit-393271.shtml

Krebs, Brian, "How Much Is Your Identity Worth?" krebsonsecurity.com, November 8, 2011. As of February 20, 2014:
http://krebsonsecurity.com/tag/fullz-info/

———, "Banking on Badb in the Underweb," krebsonsecurity.com, March 8, 2012. As of February 4, 2014:
http://krebsonsecurity.com/tag/badb-su/

———, "Crimeware Author Funds Exploit Buying Spree," krebsonsecurity.com, January 7, 2013a. As of January 7, 2013:
http://krebsonsecurity.com/2013/01/crimeware-author-funds-exploit-buying-spree/

———, "U.S. Government Seizes LibertyReserve.com," krebsonsecurity.com, May 28, 2013b. As of February 4, 2014:
http://krebsonsecurity.com/tag/libertyreserve-com-reserve-takedown/

———, "Underweb Payments, Post-Liberty Reserve," krebsonsecurity.com, May 30, 2013c. As of February 4, 2014:
http://krebsonsecurity.com/2013/05/underweb-payments-post-liberty-reserve/

———, "Styx Crypt Makers Push DDoS, Anti-Antivirus Services," krebsonsecurity.com, July 19, 2013d. As of February 4, 2014:
http://krebsonsecurity.com/tag/carder-pro/

———, Cards stolen in Target Breach Flood Underground Markets, krebsonsecurity.com, December 20, 2013e. As of February 20, 2014:
http://krebsonsecurity.com/2013/12/cards-stolen-in-target-breach-flood-underground-markets/

———, "Data Broker Giants Hacked by ID Theft Service," krebsonsecurity.com, September 25, 2013f. As of February 3, 2014:
http://krebsonsecurity.com/2013/09/data-broker-giants-hacked-by-id-theft-service/

———, "Experian Sold Consumer Data to ID Theft Service," krebsonsecurity.com, October 20, 2013g. As of February 4, 2014:
http://krebsonsecurity.com/tag/hieupc/

———, "Non-U.S. Cards Used at Target Fetch Premium," krebsonsecurity.com, December 22, 2013h. As of February 4, 2014:
http://krebsonsecurity.com/2013/12/non-us-cards-used-at-target-fetch-premium/

Kumar, Mohit, "vBulletin Forum Hacked with Zero Day Vulnerability, Caused Macrumors Forum Data Breach," thehackernews.com, November 17, 2013. As of February 4, 2014:
http://thehackernews.com/2013/11/vBulletin-hacked-Zero-Day-vulnerability.html

Lemon, Sumner, "Average Zero-Day Bug Has 348-Day Lifespan, Exec Says," networkworld.com, July 9, 2007. As of February 4, 2014:
http://www.networkworld.com/news/2007/070907-average-zero-day-bug-has-348-day.html

Leopando, Jonathan, "Blackhole Arrests—How Has the Underground Reacted?" trendmicro.com, October 21, 2013. As of November 11, 2013:
http://blog.trendmicro.com/trendlabs-security-intelligence/blackhole-arrests-how-has-the-underground-reacted/

Lewis, James, and Stewart Baker, *The Economic Impact of Cybercrime and Cyber Espionage*, Sunnyvale, Calif.: McAffe Labs and the Center for Strategic and International Studies, July 2013. As of February 3, 2014:
http://www.mcafee.com/us/resources/reports/rp-economic-impact-cybercrime.pdf

Leyden, John, "Spam Volumes Show Massive Drop—But Why?" theregister.co.uk, June 30, 2011. As of February 4, 2014:
http://www.theregister.co.uk/2011/06/30/spam_volumes_shrink/

———, "How Mystery DDoSers Tried to Take Down Bitcoin Exchange with 100Gbps Crapflood: El Reg Talks to Anti-DDos Bods—Who UNMASK the Target . . . ," *The Register/Security*, October 17, 2013a. As of February 3, 2014:
http://www.theregister.co.uk/2013/10/17/bitcoin_exchange_ddos_flood/

———, "Feds Charge Vietnamese Suspect with Slurp'n'flog of Half-a-Million Americans' ID Data," theregister.co.uk, October 22, 2013b. As of February 4, 2014:
http://www.theregister.co.uk/2013/10/22/id_fraud_data_brokering_charges/

Lion Gu, *Beyond Online Gaming Cybercrime: Revisiting the Chinese Underground Market*, Cupertineo, Calif.: Trend Micro, 2013. As of February 3, 2014:
http://www.trendmicro.com/cloud-content/us/pdfs/security-intelligence/white-papers/wp-beyond-online-gaming-cybercrime.pdf

Loidl, Jarrod, "VUPEN vs Google and the Consequences for IT Security," jarrodloidl.blogspot.com, May 22, 2011. As of February 4, 2014:
http://jarrodloidl.blogspot.com/2011/05/vupen-vs-google-and-consequences-for-it.html

M86 Security Labs, *Web Exploits: There's an App for That*, Orange, Calif.: M86 Security, 2010. As of February 3, 2014:
http://www.a51.nl/storage/pdf/m86_web_exploits_report.pdf

Magnuson, Stew, "Growing Black Market for Cyber-Attack Tools Scares Senior DoD Official," *National Defense Magazine*, February 22, 2013. As of November 11, 2013:
http://www.nationaldefensemagazine.org/blog/Lists/Posts/Post.aspx?ID=1064

Malwageddon, "LightsOut EK: 'By the Way . . . How Much Is the Fish!?'," malwageddon.blogspot.nl, September 29, 2013. As of 4 February 2014:
http://malwageddon.blogspot.nl/2013/09/unknown-ek-by-way-how-much-is-fish.html

Manly, Maria, "CryptoLocker Emergence Connected to Blackhole Exploit Kit Arrest," blog.trendmicro.com, November 8, 2013. As of February 2014:
http://blog.trendmicro.com/trendlabs-security-intelligence/cryptolocker-emergence-connected-to-blackhole-exploit-kit-arrest/

Martinez, Vicente, *Ice Pack Uncovered*, Panda Security, December 2007. As of February 3, 2014:
http://pandalabs.pandasecurity.com/blogs/images/PandaLabs/2007/12/18/Icepack.pdf

McAfee Avert Labs, "The Future of Security," *Sage*, Vol. 1, No. 2, April 2007. As of February 3, 2014:
http://www.mcafee.com/us/resources/reports/rp-mcafee-labs-sage-2007.pdf

———, "One Internet, Many Worlds," *Sage,* Vol. 2, No. 1, February 2008. As of February 3, 2014:
http://www.mcafee.com/us/resources/reports/rp-mcafee-labs-sage-2008.pdf

McAfee Labs, *McAfee Threats Report: Fourth Quarter 2009,* Santa Clara, Calif.: McAfee, Inc., 2009. As of
February 3, 2014:
http://www.mcafee.com/us/resources/reports/rp-quarterly-threat-q4-2009.pdf

———, *McAfee Threats Report: Fourth Quarter 2010,* Santa Clara, Calif.: McAfee, Inc., 2010. As of February
3, 2014: http://www.mcafee.com/us/resources/reports/rp-quarterly-threat-q4-2010.pdf_

———, *McAfee Threats Report: Fourth Quarter 2011,* Santa Clara, Calif.: McAfee, Inc., 2011. As of February
3, 2014:
http://www.mcafee.com/us/resources/reports/rp-quarterly-threat-q4-2011.pdf

———, *McAfee Threats Report: Fourth Quarter 2012,* Santa Clara, Calif.: McAfee, Inc., 2012. As of February
3, 2014:
http://www.mcafee.com/us/resources/reports/rp-quarterly-threat-q4-2012.pdf

———, *McAfee Threats Report: Second Quarter 2013,* Santa Clara, Calif.: McAfee, Inc., 2013. As of February
3, 2014:
http://www.mcafee.com/us/resources/reports/rp-quarterly-threat-q2-2013.pdf

———, *McAfee Threats Report: Third Quarter 2013,* Santa Clara, Calif.: McAfee, Inc., 2013. As of February 3,
2014:
http://www.mcafee.com/us/resources/reports/rp-quarterly-threat-q3-2013.pdf

Menn, Joseph, *Fatal System Error: The Hunt for the New Crime Lords Who Are Bringing Down the Internet,*
PublicAffairs, 2010

Miller, Charlie, *The Legitimate Vulnerability Market: Inside the Secretive World of 0-day Exploit Sales,*
Independent Security Evaluators, May 6, 2007. As of October 31, 2013:
http://weis2007.econinfosec.org/papers/29.pdf

Mimoso, Michael, "64-Bit Version of Zeus Banking Trojan in the Wild," threatpost.com, December 11, 2013.
As of February 4, 2014:
http://threatpost.com/64-bit-version-of-zeus-banking-trojan-in-the-wild/103159

Musil, Steven, "Google Beefs Up the Cash Bounty for Reporting Vulnerabilities," CNET.com, June 6, 2013.
As of November 11, 2013:
http://news.cnet.com/8301-1009_3-57588164-83/google-beefs-up-the-cash-bounty-for-reporting-vulnerabilities/

Namestnikov, Yury, "The Economics of Botnets," SecureList.com, July 22, 2009. As of February 3, 2014:
http://www.securelist.com/en/analysis?pubid=204792068

Netragard, "Zero-Day Exploit Acquisition Program," netragard.com, undated. As of February 4, 2014:
http://www.netragard.com/zero-day-exploit-acquisition-program

NibbleSecurity, "No More Free Bugs," blog.nibblesec.com, undated. As of February 4, 2014:
http://blog.nibblesec.org/2011/10/no-more-free-bugs-initiatives.html

Norton, "The Cybercrime Blackmarket," Norton.com. As of February 3, 2014:
http://us.norton.com/cybercrime-blackmarket

O'Gorman, Gavin, and Geogg McDonald, *Ransomware: A Growing Menace,* Mountain View, Calif.:
Symantec, November 2012. As of October 31, 2013:
http://www.symantec.com/content/en/us/enterprise/media/security_response/whitepapers/ransomware-a-
growing-menace.pdf

O'Harrow, Robert Jr., "Hacking Tool Kits, Available Free Online, Fuel Growing Cyberspace Arms Race,"
Washingtonpost.com, November 13, 2012. As of February 3, 2014:
http://articles.washingtonpost.com/2012-11-13/news/35504365_1_hacking-tools-hackers-metasploit

Ozment, Andy, *Bug Auctions: Vulnerability Markets Reconsidered,* presented at the Workshop on Economics
and Information Security, Minneapolis, Minn., May 13–14, 2004. As of November 11, 2013:
http://www.andyozment.com/papers/weis04-ozment-bugauc.pdf

Paganini, Pierluigi, "Zero-Day Market, the Governments Are the Main Buyers," Securityaffairs.co, May 21, 2013. As of February 3, 2014:
http://securityaffairs.co/wordpress/14561/malware/zero-day-market-governments-main-buyers.html

Paget, François, *Cybercrime and Hacktivism,* Sunnyvale, Calif.: McAfee Labs, 2010a. As of February 3, 2014:
http://www.mcafee.com/us/resources/white-papers/wp-cybercrime-hactivism.pdf

———, "An Overview of Exploit Packs," McAfee.com, May 28, 2010b. As of February 3, 2014:
http://blogs.mcafee.com/mcafee-labs/an-overview-of-exploit-packs

———, "Another Overview of Exploit Packs," McAfee.com, February 24, 2012. As of February 3, 2014:
http://blogs.mcafee.com/mcafee-labs/another-overview-of-exploit-packs

Panda Security. *The Cyber-Crime Black Market: Uncovered,* Panda Security Report, 2011. As of November 11, 2013:
http://press.pandasecurity.com/wp-content/uploads/2011/01/The-Cyber-Crime-Black-Market.pdf

Parkour, Mila, "An Overview of Exploit Packs (Update 20) Jan 2014," contagiodump.blogspot.com, January 8, 2014. As of February 4, 2014:
http://contagiodump.blogspot.com/2010/06/overview-of-exploit-packs-update.html

Pastebin.com, *Untitled,* pastebin.com, November 25, 2013. As of February 4, 2014:
http://pastebin.com/YDvDyt4Q

PC Bits, *Fraudware Alert!* web page, undated. As of February 20, 2014:
http://www.pcbitsweb.com/fraudware.html

PlugBot, status update, twitter.com, January 10, 2013. As of February 4, 2014:
https://twitter.com/theplugbot/status/289421387255390208?uid=534791054&iid=853
f2b37-8844-4887-b802-662a65553f1c&nid=12+45+20130110

Ponemon Institute, "2012 Cost of Cyber Crime Study: United States," HP Enterprise Security, October 2012. As of November 2, 2013:
http://www.ponemon.org/local/upload/file/2012_US_Cost_of_Cyber_Crime_Study_FINAL6%20.pdf

———, "2013 Cost of Cyber Crime Study: United States," HP Enterprise Security, October 2013. As of November 2, 2013:
http://media.scmagazine.com/documents/54/2013_us_ccc_report_final_6-1_13455.pdf

Porche, Isaac R. III, Chad C. Serena, Colin p. Clarke, Lillian Ablon, Muharrem Mane, Zev Winkelman, Cynthia Dion-Schwarz, Jerry M. Sollinger, R. Wayne Dudding, and Shawn McKay, *Information in Warfare and Land Cyber Operations in 2020 and Beyond*, Santa Monica, Calif.: RAND Corporation, PR-764, 2013. Not available to the general public.

Protalinski, Emil, "Security Firm VUPEN Claims to Have Hacked Windows 8 and IE10," thenextweb.com blog, November 1, 2012. As of November 11, 2013:
http://thenextweb.com/microsoft/2012/11/01/security-firm-vupen-claims-to-have-hacked-windows-8-and-ie10/

Qing, Liau Yun, "U.S. Agency Hunts Down International Cybercrime Ring," zdnet.com, January 4, 2011. As of February 4, 2014:
http://www.zdnet.com/us-agency-hunts-down-international-cybercrime-ring-2062205427/

Ramzan, Zulficar, "The Vulnerability and Exploit Market (Parts 1 & 2)," July 19, 2013. As of October 7, 2013:
http://www.youtube.com/watch?v=XrgrWCgLjPQ
http://www.youtube.com/watch?v=RqeLPpZXBc4._

Rantapelkonen, Jari, and Mirva Salminen (eds.), *The Fog of Cyber Defence*, Helsinki: National Defence University/Department of Leadership and Military Pedagogy, Series 2: Article Collection No: 10, 2013. As of November 11, 2013:
http://www.doria.fi/bitstream/handle/10024/88689/The%20Fog%20of%20Cyber%20Defence%20NDU%202013.pdf

Ritter, Ken, "Carder.su ID Theft Ring Busted; Feds Arrest 19 in 9 States," huffingtonpost.com, March 16, 2012. As of February 4, 2014:
http://www.huffingtonpost.com/2012/03/17/cardersu-id-theft-ring-busted_n_1355631.html

Rothbard, Murray, "Free Market," Library of Economics and Liberty, 2008. As of February 20, 2014:
http://www.econlib.org/library/Enc/FreeMarket.html

Rouse, Margaret, "Attack Vector," SearchSecurity.com, May 2012. As of February 3, 2014:
http://searchsecurity.techtarget.com/definition/attack-vector

Samani, Raj, and François Paget, *Cybercrime Exposed: Cybercrime-as-a-Service*, Sunnyvale, Calif.: McAfee and McAfee Labs, 2013. As of February 3, 2014:
http://www.mcafee.com/us/resources/white-papers/wp-cybercrime-exposed.pdf

Schipka, Maksym, *The Online Shadow Economy: A Billion-Dollar Market for Malware Authors*, New York: MessageLabs, 2007. As of November 11, 2013:
https://www.legis.iowa.gov/DOCS/LSA/IntComHand/2009/IHEGC012.PDF

Schneier, Bruce, "Schneier: Full Disclosure of Security Vulnerabilities a 'Damned Good Idea'," schneier.com, January 2007. As of February 2014:
https://www.schneier.com/essay-146.html

Schwartz, Mathew J., "Pssst . . . Want to Rent a Botnet?," darkreading.com, May 28, 2010. As of February 4, 2014:
http://www.darkreading.com/vulnerability/pssstwant-to-rent-a-botnet/225200525

———, "NSA Contracted with Zero-Day Vendor Vupen," informationweek.com, September 17, 2013. As of February 4, 2014:
http://www.informationweek.com/security/government/nsa-contracted-with-zero-day-vendor-vupe/240161389

Segura, Jerome, "Blackhole Exploit Kit Author Reportedly Arrested, Changes Already Noticeable," blog.malwarebytes.com, October 7, 2013. As of February 4, 2014:
http://blog.malwarebytes.org/cyber-crime/2013/10/blackhole-exploit-kit-author-reportedly-arrested-changes-already-noticeable/

Shankland, Stephen, "Google Pays Bug Hunters for Finding Windows Flaw," CNET.com, September 26, 2012. As of November 11, 2013:
 http://news.cnet.com/8301-1023_3-57520440-93/google-pays-bug-hunters-for-finding-windows-flaw/

Shim, Woohyun, Luca Allodi, and Fabio Massacci, *Crime Pays if You Are Just an Average Hacker*, conference proceedings, IEEE/ASE Cyber Security Conference, 2012; Complementary publication in ASE Journal 2012, Vol. 2.; presented at the 2012 CyberSecurity Conference in Alexandria, Va., December 16, 2012. As of November 2, 2013:
http://disi.unitn.it/~allodi/shim-12-cybersecurity.pdf and https://securitylab.disi.unitn.it/lib/exe/fetch.php?media=cybersec-12.pdf

Social-Engineer.org, homepage, undated. As of February 20, 2014:
http://www.social-engineer.org/

Sophos, "Spyware Kits Sold for $15 Available on the Web, Sophos Reports," Sophos.com, March 24, 2006. As of February 4, 2014:
http://www.sophos.com/en-us/press-office/press-releases/2006/03/russianspykits.aspx

Symantec, *Symantec Intelligence Report: June 2011*. As of February 4, 2014:
http://www.symantec.com/content/en/us/about/media/pdfs/symc_intelligence_report_june2011.pdf

———, "Grappling with the ZeroAccess Botnet," Symantec.com, September 30, 2013. As of February 3, 2014:
http://www.symantec.com/connect/blogs/grappling-zeroaccess-botnet

Tarakanov, Dmitry, "ZeuS on the Hunt," SecureList.com, April 12, 2010. As of February 3, 2014:
http://www.securelist.com/en/analysis/204792107/ZeuS_on_the_Hunt

Techopedia, *Bug Bounty*, web page, undated-a. As of February 20, 2014:
http://www.techopedia.com/definition/28637/bug-bounty

———, *Obfuscator*, web page, undated-b. As of February 20, 2014:
http://www.techopedia.com/definition/21085/obfuscator

————, *Payload*, web page, undated-c. As of February 20, 2014:
http://www.techopedia.com/definition/5381/payload

TechTarget.com, SearchCloudComputing, *XaaS (Anything as a Service)*, web page, August 2010. As of February 20, 2014:
http://searchcloudcomputing.techtarget.com/definition/XaaS-anything-as-a-service

————, SearchSecurity, *Attack Vector*, May 2012. As of February 20, 2014:
http://searchsecurity.techtarget.com/definition/attack-vector

Thomas, K., D. McCoy, C. Grier, A. Kolcz, and V. Paxson, *Trafficking Fraudulent Accounts: The Role of the Underground Market in Twitter Spam and Abuse*, proceedings of the 22nd Annual USENIX Security Symposium (Usenix Sec 2013), Washington D.C., August 2013. As of October 31, 2013:
http://www.icir.org/vern/papers/twitter-acct-purch.usesec13.pdf

United States of America vs [redacted], et al. No. 12-2359-TEB, January 10, 2012. As of February 4, 2014:
http://www.cis.uab.edu/forensics/blog/Kostyukov.Indictment.pdf

Vbulletin, Forums, Topics, and Posts, web page, undated. As of February 20, 2014:
http://www.vbulletin.com/forum/help?faq=vb3_board_usage#faq_vb3_forums_threads_posts; http://en.wikipedia.org/wiki/Internet_forum

WabiSabiLabi, "Squeezing the Lemon Twice," wabisabilabi.blogspot.com, July 10, 2007. As of February 4, 2014:
http://wabisabilabi.blogspot.com/2007/07/squeezing-lemon-twice.html

Warner, Gary, "Carders Do Battle Through Spam—Carder.su," garwarner.blogspot.com, March 18, 2009. As of February 4, 2014:
http://garwarner.blogspot.com/2009/03/carders-do-battle-through-spam-cardersu.html

————, "Operation Open Market: The Vendors," garwarner.blogspot.com, March 25, 2012. As of February 4, 2014:
http://garwarner.blogspot.com/2012/03/operation-open-market-vendors.html

Webopedia, *DDoS Attack—Distributed Denial of Service*, web page, undated-a. As of February 20, 2014:
http://www.webopedia.com/TERM/D/DDoS_attack.html

————, *Spam*, web page, undated-b. As of February 20, 2014:
http://www.webopedia.com/TERM/S/spam.html

————, *Spyware*, web page, undated-c. As of February 20, 2014:
http://www.webopedia.com/TERM/S/spyware.html

West Coast Labs, "Malware & Security Threat Glossary," WestCoastLabs.com, undated. As of February 3, 2014:
http://www.westcoastlabs.com/checkmark/glossary/

West's Encyclopedia of American Law, "Fungible," Detroit: Thomson/Gale, 2008.

White, Charlie, "Spam Decreased 82.22 Percent Over the Past Year," mashable.com, July 3, 2011. As of February 4, 2014:
http://mashable.com/2011/07/03/spam-decreased-82percent/

Wikipedia, *Broker*, web page, updated February 23, 2014a. As of February 20, 2014:
http:/en.wikipedia.org/wiki/Cryptocurrency

————, *Cryptocurrency*, web page, updated February 19, 2014b. As of February 20, 2014:
http:/en.wikipedia.org/wiki/Cryptocurrency

————, *Data Breach*, web page, updated February 16, 2014b. As of February 20, 2014:
http://en.wikipedia.org/wiki/Data_breach

————, *Deep Web*, web page, updated February 19, 2014c. As of February 20, 2014:
http://en.wikipedia.org/wiki/Deep_web

————, *Digital Currency*, updated February 7, 2014d. As of February 20, 2014:
http://en.wikipedia.org/wiki/Digital_currency

———, *E-commerce*, web page, updated Febrary 20, 2014e. As of February 20, 2014:
http://en.wikipedia.org/wiki/E-commerce

———, *Encryption*, web page, updated February 18, 2014f. As of February 20, 2014:
http://en.wikipedia.org/wiki/Encryption

———, *Hacktivism*, web page, modified February 19, 2014g. As of February 20, 2014:
http://en.wikipedia.org/wiki/Hacktivism

———, *Instant Messaging*, web page, modified January 30, 2014h. As of February 20, 2014:
http://en.wikipedia.org/wiki/Instant_messaging

———, *Intellectual Property*, web page, modified February 16, 2014i. As of February 20, 2014:
http://en.wikipedia.org/wiki/Intellectual_property

———, *Malware*, web page, modified February 16, 2014j. As of February 14, 2014j:
http://en.wikipedia.org/wiki/Malware

———, *Off-the-Record Messaging*, web page, modified February 16, 2014k. As of February 14, 2014j:
http://en.wikipedia.org/wiki/Off-the-Record_Messaging

———, *Peer-to-Peer*, web page, modified February 19, 2014k. as of February 20, 2014:
http://en.wikipedia.org/wiki/Peer-to-peer

———, *Phishing*, web page, modified February 11, 2014l, As of February 20, 2014:
http://en.wikipedia.org/wiki/Phishing

———, *Point of Sale*, web page, modified February 20, 2014m, As of February 20, 2014:
http://en.wikipedia.org/wiki/Point_of_sale

———, *Product (Business)*, web page, modified February 17, 2014n, As of February 20, 2014:
http://en.wikipedia.org/wiki/Product_(business)

———, *Ransomware*, web page, modified, February 19, 2014o. As of February 20, 2014:
http://en.wikipedia.org/wiki/Ransomware_(malware)

———, *Search Engine Optimization*, web page, modified January 29, 2014p. As of February 20, 2014:
http://en.wikipedia.org/wiki/Search_engine_optimization

———, *Spamming*, web page, modified February 20, 2014q. As of February 20, 2014:
http://en.wikipedia.org/wiki/Spamming

———, *Tor (Anonymity Network)*, web page, modified February 19, 2014r. As of February 20, 2014:
http://en.wikipedia.org/wiki/Tor_(anonymity_network)

———, *Virtual Machine*, web page, modified February 19, 2014s. As of February 20, 2014:
http://en.wikipedia.org/wiki/Virtual_machine

———, *Virtual Private Network*, web page, modified February 15, 2014t. As of February 20, 2014:
http://en.wikipedia.org/wiki/Virtual_private_network

———, *Zeus (Trojan horse)*, web page, modified January 30, 2014u. As of February 20, 2014:
http://en.wikipedia.org/wiki/Virtual_private_network

Zeltser, Lenny, "What Are Exploit Kits?" blog.zeltser.com, October 26, 2010. As of February 6, 2014:
http://blog.zeltser.com/post/1410922437/what-are-exploit-kits

Zetter, Kim, "Google Offers $1 Million in Hacker Bounties for Exploits Against Chrome," wired.com, February 28, 2012a. As of November 11, 2013:
http://www.wired.com/threatlevel/2012/02/google-1-million-dollar-hack-contest/

———, "Portrait of a Full-Time Bug Hunter—Abdul-Aziz Hariri," Wired.com, November 8, 2012b. As of November 11, 2013:
http://www.wired.com/threatlevel/2012/11/bug-hunting/

———, "Microsoft Launches $100K Bug Bounty Program," Wired.com, June 19, 2013. As of November 11, 2013:
http://www.wired.com/threatlevel/2013/06/microsoft-bug-bounty-program/

Zheng, Bu, Pedro Bueno, Rahul Kashyap, and Adam Wosotowsky, *The New Era of Botnets*, Sunnyvale, Calif.: McAfee Labs, 2010. As of February 3, 2014:
http://www.mcafee.com/us/resources/white-papers/wp-new-era-of-botnets.pdf

Selected Interviews and Personal Communications

Adams, Kyle, Juniper Networks, email communication with the authors, October 2013.

Allodi, Luca, Università degli Studi di Trento, telephone interview with the authors, October 2013.

Clinton, Larry, President of Internet Security Alliance, telephone interview with the authors, December 2013.

Fidler, Mailyn, email communication with the authors, January 2014.

Guido, Dan, CEO of Trail of Bits, telephone interview with the authors, October 2013.

Helm, Fred, Senior Manager, Asset Protection, of WalMart Corp., telephone interview with the authors, November 2013.

Howard, Rick, CSO of Palo Alto Networks, email communication with the authors, October 2013.

Huston, Brent, MicroSolved, telephone interview with the authors, October 2013.

McAllister, Sean, Accuvant Software Security Group, email communication with the authors, October 2013.

Marcus, Dave, McAfee Labs, telephone interview with the authors, December 2013.

Menn, Joseph, investigative reporter and author of the book *Fatal System Error*, telephone interview with the authors, November 2013.

Paget, François, McAfee Labs, email communication with the authors, December 2013–February 2014.

Parkour, Mila, Contagio, email communication with the authors, November 2013–February 2014.

Paxson, Vern, University of California, Berkeley, and International Computer Science Institute, email communication with the authors, November 2013.

Plesco, Ron, KPMG, telephone interview with the authors, December 2013.

Ponemon, Larry, Ponemon Institute, telephone interview with the authors, November 2013.

Reynolds, Ted, Professor at University of Central Florida, telephone interview with the authors, October 2013.

BitcoinShop, Inc. representative, telephone interview with the authors, October 2013 (name withheld on request).

Vennon, Troy, Juniper Networks, telephone interview with the authors, October 2013.

Watson, Alex, Director of Security Research at Websense, email communication with the authors, October 2013.

As noted earlier, we also spoke with those who wish to remain anonymous. These include six law enforcement/ government personnel and two security researchers.